FROM MANAGING TO EMPOWERING

An ACTION GUIDE to Developing Winning FACILITATION Skills

FROM MANAGING TO EMPOWERING

An ACTION GUIDE to Developing Winning FACILITATION Skills

SCOTT B. PARRY

QUALITY RESOURCES®
A Division of The Kraus Organization Limited
902 Broadway, New York, New York 10010

Most Quality Resources books are available at quantity discounts when purchased in bulk. For more information contact:

Special Sales Department
Quality Resources
A Division of The Kraus Organization Limited
902 Broadway
New York, New York 10010
800-247-8519   (212) 979-8600

Copyright © 1994 Scott B. Parry

All rights reserved. No part of this work covered by the copyrights hereon may be reproduced or used in any form or by any means—graphic, electronic, or mechanical, including photocopying, recording, taping, or information storage and retrieval systems—without written permission of the publisher.

Printed in the United States of America

98 97 96 95   10 9 8 7 6 5 4 3 2

Quality Resources
A Division of The Kraus Organization Limited
902 Broadway
New York, New York 10010
(212) 979-8600
800-247-8519

The paper used in this publication meets the minimum requirements of American National Standards for Information Sciences—Permanence of Paper for Printed Library Materials, ANSI Z39.48-1984.

ISBN 0-527-76232-6

Library of Congress Cataloging-in-Publication Data

Parry, Scott B.
   From managing to empowering : an action guide to developing winning facilitation skills / Scott B. Parry.
     p. cm.
   Includes index.
   ISBN 0-527-76232-6 (alk. paper)
   1. Communication in small groups. 2. Group relations training. 3. Work groups. I. Title.
HM133.P36 1994
302.3'4—dc20   93-47184
                                                                                CI

Table of Contents

	Pages
Introduction	vii
Chapter 1. Empowerment and Facilitation	1
Self-Quiz	6
Chapter 2. Your Response Style	9
Self-Quiz	20
Chapter 3. Changing the Corporate Culture	23
Self-Quiz	32
Chapter 4. Discussion Leadership Skills	35
Self-Quiz	45
Chapter 5. Using Questions Effectively	49
Self-Quiz	58
Chapter 6. Roles and Responsibilities	67
Self-Quiz	81
Chapter 7. Making Work Teams Work	85
Self-Quiz	104
Chapter 8. Meeting Leadership	107
Self-Quiz	119
Chapter 9. Training and Development	121
Self-Quiz	131
Chapter 10. Coaching and Counseling	133
Self-Quiz	139

Chapter 11. Analyzing and Solving Problems	**143**
Self-Quiz	148
Chapter 12: Making Decisions	**151**
Self-Quiz	161
Appendix	**165**
Process Skills for Facilitators	165
Guidelines for Group Behavior in Meetings	167
Sample Response Sheet (Training Session)	169
A Facilitator's Creed	172
Meeting Announcement/Agenda	173
Meeting Recap (Follow up Minutes)	174
Coaching and Counseling Planning Sheet (Rudy's Example)	175
A Team Member's Creed	179
Index	**181**

Introduction

Empowerment is in. Motivation is out. The motivation school of management tried to manipulate the physical and psychological variables that we believed would get employees to work harder, better, smarter, faster, safer, or whatever. This approach has been less than successful. The missing ingredient: power. The finest physical environment, employee benefits, and human relations programs will not motivate a powerless employee.

As we prepare for a new millennium, the empowerment school of management is emerging as the way to build a world-class organization. This book explains the tools, techniques, concepts, and skills needed to make empowerment work. Empowerment works when all employees become managers of their own time and talent, their supervisors become mentors rather than tormentors, everyone agrees on how to spell quality and service, and interactions move from parent-child to adult-adult relationships.

After a century of establishing elaborate systems to limit the power of employees, large and small corporations are doing an about face and attempting to empower their employees. Self-directed teams, employee involvement, and total quality management are all forms of empowerment.

Power is simply the ability to get things done. In physics, politics, electricity, and the world of work, when we empower individuals or organizations, we increase their ability to get things done.

Three major processes are essential to empowerment:

- The education, training, coaching, and mentoring of individuals, which is usually referred to as human resources development (HRD).
- The restructuring of working relationships, with multiple roles and memberships in partnerships, teams, task forces, and study groups.
- The transformation of the organization from bureaucracy to matrix, from restrictive to releasing, and from parent-child to adult-adult.

The term *empowerment* usually connotes a macro view of these processes. I prefer to focus on the micro view—that is, the facilitation skills that team leaders, supervisors, managers, human resources development (HRD) specialists, and others need to make empowerment a reality.

This book has been a learning odyssey for me. I've broken the three processes noted above into a dozen chapters that spell out the tools, techniques, concepts, and skills I've learned in working with such firms as Ford, IBM, Budd, Shell, Burns, and PSE&G. They are as much my mentors as my clients, and my gratitude runs deep.

We'll begin with an exploration of the role and expectations of a facilitator (chapter 1), followed by an assessment of your style in responding to situations (chapter 2) and an interpretation of the implication of your scores as they relate to the culture of your organization (chapter 3).

Because group process skills are the facilitator's major stock in trade, we'll address your ability to lead discussions, use questions effectively, and deal with group dynamics effectively (chapters 4 through 6). You'll evaluate 35 key issues that work teams have had to deal with (chapter 7), and you'll learn how to provide effective leadership at meetings (chapter 8).

The remaining four topics deal with skills that facilitators are often called on to provide: training and development (chapter 9), coaching and counseling (chapter 10), problem solving (chapter 11), and decision making (chapter 12).

A self-quiz follows each chapter and is your chance to explore how you will apply the key concepts and skills with your own work groups. Finally, an appendix contains forms and checklists that you may find useful.

I've enjoyed preparing this book. May your odyssey be as rewarding as mine has been!

Scott B. Parry, Ph.D.
Princeton, NJ 1993

Empowerment And Facilitation

The internal relationships and links between work groups (e.g., departments, functions, or teams) that were once the domain of supervisors to plan, schedule, direct, and control (the management cycle) are rapidly becoming the responsibility of every employee. It's called empowerment, and facilitation skills are the key to making it work.

A century ago, all you needed to become a supervisor was the ability to perform every job or task in your work unit and do it better than the employees who were hired to do these jobs. Half a century ago, we learned that the role of supervisor was to get work done through others, without necessarily being able to do it yourself (much less being able to do it better yourself). Today's sociotechnical workplace has evolved even further, for example:

- Many employees are specialists who are expected to manage their time, talent, and resources, often without immediate access to a manager.
- Many supervisors and managers are expected to get things done through employees who are not subordinates and who have other priorities.
- Many work groups are learning how to function as self-directed teams, with relatively little direct supervision.

In short, employees are becoming their own supervisors, getting work done alone or with help from others, and cultivating the links needed to do so. These employees, like their managers, must also win the cooperation of people who have other priorities and who owe them no allegiance. There are no subordinates in an empowered organization.

I've used facilitation skills to describe the tools and techniques that employees need to get work done in alliance with others. Pages 165 through 168 in the Appendix list the 20 skills we'll be discussing. Take a few minutes now to see how many of these are important to your job. (If the majority do not apply, you may not need to continue with this program.)

Successful completion of chapter 1 can be measured by the degree to which you meet the following objectives. You should be able to:

- Give at least five reasons empowerment is gaining popularity.
- Define the role of facilitator, based on the root meaning of the work.
- Show how individual styles and attitudes relate to the company's climate and culture.
- Describe the two types of parent-to-child interactions, using examples of each.
- Define TQM, SDT, HRD, and Theory X and Y.
- List four categories of change agents that require facilitation skills.
- Identify at least six facilitation skills that are important to your success at work.

Open any newspaper or journal and you'll find at least a dozen commonly used words, phrases, or abbreviations that were not part of our business vocabulary a decade ago. I'm thinking of words like *empowerment, total quality management* (TQM), *stakeholders, self-directed teams* (SDTs), *champions, mentoring, continuous improvement programs* (CIPs), *benchmarking,* and *facilitators*.

These terms reflect a revolutionary change in the way organizations do business and deal with people, both internally (employees) and externally (customers and suppliers). Facilitation skills are increasingly important if empowerment is to become a permanent reality in the new millennium and not just a passing fad or buzzword of the 1990s.

In simplest terms, a facilitator makes it easier for others to perform work more effectively. (The Latin word *facilitas* means easiness.) Empowerment is the process of releasing and conferring power so that people can perform their work more effectively. We can conclude that facilitators are the people who make the process of empowerment work. Facilitators are empowerers.

Where are these facilitators found in the empowered organization? Is it a position one interviews for? Do job descriptions exist? Is it part of a specific career path? Certainly not. The role of facilitators is not a box on the organization chart. Rather, facilitation skills are the daily tools used by a variety of change agents found throughout any organization. They include:

- Managers and supervisors who are learning that being a boss is not as effective as being a coach.
- Staff specialists from Human Resources Development (HRD) who are learning how to help their internal clients solve problems and make decisions themselves rather than providing pat answers.
- Leaders of self-directed teams, whose ability to release the energy and

creativity of members depends on process skills more than on content expertise.
- Employees who have learned that they are far more effective when they listen, show understanding, and ask thought-provoking questions than when they criticize, give advice, and allow parent-to-child interactions to supplant adult-to-adult relationships.

Facilitation skills and empowerment are not just updated terms for the human relations movement of the 1950s and 1960s with its themes of "Employee's aren't hired hands" or "Be nice to people and they'll be more productive and less contentious."

Empowerment and facilitation skills are critical to the success of organizations that operate in a global economy. In a world of overnight changes in technology, legislation, competition, employees, customers, and market demands, the bureaucratic organization chart and autocratic ways of doing business are no longer effective. A massive overhaul in the culture of the organization is essential to its success—perhaps even to its survival.

Think of the organization as a ship. For centuries, the ship has been churning ahead in one direction. Officers (managers) made all the decisions, and the crew (workers) carried them out. Both parties seemed satisfied, which was mostly due to differences in their education and status.

But now the leveling of differences in education and socioeconomic status has made the line between managers and workers a thin one. Most organizations genuinely want to see every employee functioning as a manager—that is, seeing their time as something to be invested, not merely spent, seeing their work as a career, not just a job, and seeing continuous improvement as a commitment, not a fad.

Other major factors have recently made it desirable and indeed, essential for organizations to empower their employees; they include:

- Concern for employee satisfaction, fulfillment, and the quality of work life.
- The mentoring of new employees, driven by increasing diversity in the work force.
- The desire of organizations to become a learning enterprise.
- The quest for total quality management (TQM) as every employee's responsibility.
- Benchmarking against best practices to chart continuous improvement (*Kaizen*).
- The thinning of the organization chart—that is, fewer middle managers.
- Concern about the work environment and the organization's role as a champion.
- The need to make employee involvement a reality and not a fad.
- The realization that employees in other cultures have been outperforming our own.

In short, our ship has entered new waters, and this has forced the officers to change the course their ship has been on for centuries and to move toward a new objective: making every employee a manager of their own time and talent.

Turning a ship the size of an organization requires tremendous effort from everyone on board. Hence empowerment. It's a means of releasing and harnessing the full power that lies within each employee.

However, the process of turning a huge ship is sometimes barely perceptible to those on board. Moreover, it often takes a lot more time than anyone would expect. So the move to empowerment and the realignment of goals and priorities is met with frustration, uncertainty, suspicion, and distrust. These attitudes are common to officers and crew alike when entering new waters.

The culture of the ship, like that of most organizations, has been characterized by parent-to-child interactions between officers and crew. Sometimes the relationship was benevolent paternalism. Sometimes it was authoritarian and oppressive.

Douglas McGregor labeled these two parental styles Soft and Hard Theory X. Both kinds of management treat employees like children. Indeed, the primary characteristic of a Theory X, parent-to-child organizational culture is that workers have been viewed as hired hands who were paid to carry out orders but not to think for themselves. Employees were often punished for making decisions or attempting to solve problems. This was the work of managers, acting in response to one of two sets of beliefs:

- The workers aren't ready to assume higher levels of responsibility. We must do it for them. (This is the Soft X, benevolent parent, under whom the employees will never develop and outgrow their childhood.)
- The workers will make mistakes or be lazy and unproductive unless we provide constant supervision. (This is the the Hard X, autocratic parent, whom the employees are likely to rebel against and act as misbehaving children.)

What can an organization do to foster teamwork and ensure that empowerment is an ongoing process of growth and not a fad that will pass? What can the captain do to turn the ship in a way that will dispel much of the suspicion and distrust that accompanies most any major organizational change?

They and we have no less a job than to transform the climate and culture of the organization, which is nothing more than the collective product of the individual styles and attitudes of its members. How? By easing change rather than forcing it and by releasing employees from the child role of dependency that they've been conditioned to accept. In short, by developing and modeling a facilitative style in all that we do.

Many workshops that teach facilitation skills have recently emerged. The following examples illustrate the variety of their applications in leading organizations:

- At Ford in Dearborn, MI, cross-functional teams are designing cars that will roll into dealerships in 40 to 48 months. Several years ago, it took 60 to 72 months to go from concept to customer (Ford's CTC program). Design teams (about 25 per new vehicle) have made the difference. Each team has two leaders: the content leader, an engineer and technical expert, and the process leader, a facilitator who maintains healthy relationships within and between teams.
- At Coca-Cola Companies, the production team is responsible for running the bottling line and building an inventory to meet the sales forecasts. At some bottling plants, team members and their facilitator set up the weekly production schedule so that they can take a three-day weekend if they have met the forecasted inventory levels by Thursday evening.
- At Brush Wellman in Cleveland, OH, employees had received training in TQM, and statistical process control (SPC), but improvement fell short of expectations. Howard George, the corporate manager of training and development, realized that the old guard of management was not giving empowerment a chance to work. He installed an assessment program (MAP) that measured their engineers before and after a training program that taught facilitation skills (EXCEL). From 1987 to 1990 their parent-child style dropped 15% and adult-adult style rose 74% on national norms used to benchmark performance.
- At IBM's Corporate Education Center in Thornwood, NY, managers are brought in from locations throughout the country to learn how to serve as LEAP (Leading Edge Action Program) facilitators. After several weeks of intensive training, they return to their offices and plants where they contract with work teams and project managers to help them take the actions need to make the transition, or culture shift, in the way IBM employees deal with customers and with one another. These actions are critical to the company's reorganization into 13 autonomous companies.
- At Boeing's Support Services Department in Renton, WA, a three-day program of evaluation, interpretation, and action planning is helping Boeing managers to identify the changes needed in styles, values, and competencies as they shift from autocratic supervision to a facilitator role that is more appropriate to providing team leadership. As one quality manager put it, "If we expect managers to lead the quality movement, we'd better provide them with the education and development to apply TQM in their daily lives. Unless they're living it day to day, it's only going to be perceived as lip service."
- At Public Service Electric and Gas (PSE&G) in Newark, NJ, supervisors in their generating stations are selected and developed on the basis of their proficiency on a dozen competencies and styles (values) that are

embodied in the organization's policies on teamwork and empowerment, PSE&G is a leader among utilities in making work teams successful. The criteria used to select and develop members of the supervisory teams are the result of a two-year study that identified the critical competencies needed to perform as facilitators of organizational change.
- At General Electric, Chairman Jack Welch has made it known that "GE cannot afford management styles that suppress and intimidate." The two qualities that determine whether managers can expect promotion or derailment are: the ability to deliver on commitment and shared values, style, and beliefs. In short, the ability to develop others and facilitate change. GE's management development programs systematically sharpen these skills.

In the Appendix, you'll find a list of 20 process skills for facilitators, along with two columns in which you can rate the relevancy of each to your job and your proficiency in it. Like the Facilitator's Creed, which provides a concise definition of the values and skills displayed by facilitators, this list of skills helps in defining the role of facilitator by identifying key behaviors. As you compare these behavioral descriptions with the activities that fill your workday, you'll be able to answer this question: Is facilitator a new word or a new function?

The word *facilitator* has roots that are centuries old, and you may have been successfully applying some of the skills on the list for years. Others are relatively new, however, and organizations committed to programs of quality, empowerment, and teamwork are discovering the importance of these skills. This book should help you make the same discovery and strengthen your effectiveness as a facilitator.

Self-Quiz on Empowerment and Facilitation

1. What are some of the reasons empowerment is gaining popularity? List at least five.

2. How does the Latin root of the word *facilitator* pertain to facilitation skills and the role of a facilitator?

3. What is the relationship between the style and attitudes of managers and the organization's climate and culture?

4. Give an example of the two types of parent-to-child interactions found in all organizations (i.e., McGregor's Soft Theory X and Hard Theory X)

5. What do each of these abbreviations stand for?

    TQM:

    SDT:

    HRD:

    Theory X and Y:

6. What are four categories of change agents in empowered organizations (i.e., the people that require facilitation skills)?

7. Which facilitation skills (from the list of process skills in the Appendix) are most important to your success at work?

Your Response Style

In an empowered organization, the climate and culture undergo dramatic changes. Because an organization's climate is nothing more than the cumulative styles and attitudes of its employees, the progress of any program of empowerment (e.g., team building or TQM) can be evaluated by measuring changes in style and attitude along the way. In this chapter, we'll establish the starting point.

People perform the way they do because of what they know (knowledge), how they feel (attitudes), and what abilities they possess (skills). Addressing all three ingredients is essential if we want employees to perform effectively on the job.

Many training programs relating to employee involvement, TQM, and team building focus heavily on knowledge and skills but fail to measure the attitudes of managers and employees—that is, the styles, values, feelings, beliefs, and opinions that are so important to the success of empowerment.

The self-assessment exercise in this chapter will enable you to identify your style and attitudes in your interactions with others. We can then interpret your ratings on this self-scored assessment and see how they relate to your role as a facilitator.

Upon completing chapter 2, you should be able to:

- Describe and illustrate the four response styles (E, C, S, A).
- Identify the persons with whom your relationship is parent-child and adult-adult (P-C and A-A).
- Indicate how and under what conditions the relationships might profitably be changed.

- State the implications of your ratio on the two sets of scores, P-C and A-A.
- Estimate the direction and role of change of the climate and culture (i.e., management style) of your organization.
- Determine the conditions under which a parent-to-child relationship is appropriate between managers and employees.
- Describe the types of action you and your organization might take to make the culture more supportive of teamwork and empowerment.

This self-assessment is designed to give you insight into the ways in which you respond to people. There are twelve episodes or situations to which you will respond. In each case, someone whom you know well is speaking to you. Their comments are followed by four alternative responses that you might make in reply. Your job is to rank the responses according to their appropriateness:

Give a 4 to the response that you like most.
Give a 3 to the response that you like next to most.
Give a 2 to the response that you like next to least.
Give a 1 to the response that you like least.

STATEMENT: Someone says	RESPONSE: How you might reply	
I've noticed that very few people are good listeners. They interrupt me, or ask questions later about something I just told them.	A. Maybe your message or manner of delivery doesn't interest them.	
	B. Why do you think that listening is such a difficult skill for so many people?	
	C. Perhaps you could ask them what they think from time to time . . . to keep them involved.	
	D. That can be very frustrating when people don't even give you a fair hearing.	

Figure 2.1

Your answers should be entered in the square boxes to the right of the RESPONSES (see Figure 2.1). You will probably find it easier to select your "like most" (4) and "like least" (1) responses, then decide for the remaining two selections which is better (3) and which is not (2).

In some of the items, you might not like any of the responses and would have said something quite different from the four choices we've given you. We are still asking you to rank the four options according to your idea of the relative appropriateness of each. Remember that on each statement, you can only assign each rating once—only one 4, one 3, one 2, and one 1.

Your Response Style

	STATEMENT: Someone says	RESPONSE: How you might reply	
1	I like the new system my bank just put in. Instead of separate lines for each teller, there is one waiting line, like the airlines do at their ticket counters. That way, everyone gets waited on in turn.	A. So you feel that everyone gets a fairer deal, with no one getting stuck in the slowest line?	
		B. Have you asked the tellers what the reaction to the new system has been?	
		C. They should have done that years ago, but banks are so slow to innovate.	
		D. Why don't you compliment the tellers or branch manager on the new system?	

	STATEMENT: Someone says	RESPONSE: How you might reply	
2	My daughter has been going with this guy for less than six months, and now she wants to marry him. He works nights. She makes more than he does. They seem to think that you can live on love.	A. Take care not to let your concerns turn her against you; she needs understanding, not advice.	
		B. Has she shared her feelings and reasons with you or thought the decision through?	
		C. It doesn't matter who makes more money; you shouldn't make that an issue.	
		D. You seem concerned that she's making a decision too quickly without considering all the factors.	

	STATEMENT: Someone says	RESPONSE: How you might reply	
3	I don't know what kind of personal computer to buy for home. I want one for business, but the kids want to play games on it, and I can see this keeping them from doing their homework.	A. You could set a rule: No PC games until they have done their homework.	
		B. Can you get one PC that will handle your business needs and play games for the kids?	
		C. Then you would like to accommodate the kids if it didn't interfere with their homework.	
		D. You're making a mistake to put your kid's pleasures ahead of your own business needs.	

	STATEMENT: Someone says	RESPONSE: How you might reply	
4	I'm thinking of volunteering to help on John Simms' reelection campaign. He's done a good job and deserves another term. But my husband doesn't like the idea of my getting mixed up in politics.	A. How much of your time do you think his reelection campaign will take?	
		B. Tell him that the strength of a democracy depends on people participating in it.	
		C. You'd like to work on the campaign, but don't want to upset your husband.	
		D. Your husband has no right to interfere in your working on the campaign.	

	STATEMENT: Someone says	RESPONSE: How you might reply	
5	My boss has just given me an assignment that I feel is a waste of time. My work is 90% interesting, but this new project she gave me just doesn't make sense.	A. If your job is generally interesting, it's better not to rock the boat over one project.	
		B. If it's a project you accepted, you have no right to complain about it now.	
		C. Is she open to listening to your views on the value of the project?	
		D. You're really having trouble accepting this new assignment, aren't you?	

	STATEMENT: Someone says	RESPONSE: How you might reply	
6	This morning I overheard some workers talking about our firm being acquired by a big holding company. I wonder what changes this would bring and whether I'd be as happy in my work.	A. I gather the talk you overheard this morning was a little unsettling.	
		B. Has anything been announced officially about a possible acquisition?	
		C. Don't worry, things often work out better for both parties.	
		D. You shouldn't concern yourself with gossip or rumor unless you see a factual basis for it.	

	STATEMENT: Someone says	RESPONSE: How you might reply	
7	Our overtime system is being abused right and left. Supervisors are letting their people book the extra hours to make up for the current freeze on salary increases, and they can do all the work without it.	A. People never seem to learn the danger of biting the hand that feeds them.	
		B. I'd suggest that all overtime be approved by the supervisor's manager.	
		C. Have you compared current figures with overtime figures before the freeze?	
		D. It sounds to me like you're pretty annoyed to see the system being abused.	

	STATEMENT: Someone says	RESPONSE: How you might reply	
8	I'd like to ask Dad if I can borrow the car Friday night. But after that dent I got last week, I don't think he'll let me. I repaired the dent, but his confidence in my driving may never be repaired.	A. If you hadn't put a dent in the car, you wouldn't be in this fix now, would you?	
		B. What makes you think that your dad has lost confidence in you?	
		C. Then are you concerned about your dad's confidence as well as his permission?	
		D. Could you remind him that you did fix the dent and will be fully responsible?	

Your Response Style

	STATEMENT: Someone says	RESPONSE: How you might reply	
9	My husband's got a great job and is making good money now, but he's thinking of getting a law degree. And I just read that 40% of lawyers are unhappy with their work. I don't know what to tell him.	A. I suggest that he talk to some other people, maybe even a career counselor.	
		B. Are you afraid that he won't be any better off with a law degree than he is now?	
		C. What right do you have to stand in the way of what he wants and believes in?	
		D. Has he talked with you about his reasons for wanting to pick up a law degree?	

	STATEMENT: Someone says	RESPONSE: How you might reply	
10	Can you lend me $50 for the weekend? Lee and I are going into the city and we're a bit short. I know it's more than I've borrowed in the past but I've always made good, and I'll pay you back on payday.	A. Do you think you'll be able to repay the loan in full by next payday?	
		B. If you had a savings account and put money aside regularly, you wouldn't have to borrow.	
		C. I know how frustrating it can be when you run short of money, especially before a big weekend.	
		D. Have you considered getting a cash advance on your credit card?	

	STATEMENT: Someone says	RESPONSE: How you might reply	
11	One of my students in the night course I teach never does his homework and does not participate in class. Yet he gets good grades on the tests. So I don't know what to do.	A. Have you talked with him or tried to find out why he's not participating?	
		B. Perhaps you should remind him that there's more to passing your course than just getting grades on test.	
		C. You're the one who's to blame for letting him get away with it. You should have talked to him long ago.	
		D. So you're at a loss to know why he's not responding and how to turn him on.	

	STATEMENT: Someone says	RESPONSE: How you might reply	
12	The repairman for the copy machine tells me that the drum is permanently scratched. Someone is leaving paper clips on top of the machine, despite the notice I put there. He found clips inside.	A. Some people just can't read or follow simple instructions, no matter how conspicuous you make them.	
		B. Are the scratches really making the copies look bad, or are they fairly inconspicuous?	
		C. I'd suggest that you try to find out who is responsible to avoid future problems.	
		D. That must be a bit annoying after you took the trouble to put up a notice.	

Scoring Instructions

In each set of four responses, one was critical (C), one was advising (A), one was searching for more information (S), and one showed empathy (E). To score your responses, place these four letters beside the boxes in each of the 12 items, as follows

1. E 2. A 3. A 4. S 5. A 6. E 7. C 8. C 9. A 10. S 11. S 12. C
   S   S   S   A   C   S   A   S   E   C   A   S
   C   C   E   E   S   A   S   E   C   E   C   A
   A   E   C   C   E   C   E   A   S   A   E   E

Now you are ready to add up the points you assigned to each of these four types of responses. Let's start with E. Add up the numbers in the 12 boxes that you've just printed an E beside. Enter this total in the tally box printed below.

Repeat this procedure for the 12 boxes labeled C. Enter this total in the tally box. Then do the same for the other two letters, S and A. Check to make sure your four totals add up to 120 points.

```
Tally Box

Total of all 12 E boxes (Empathic)        _____ points

Total of all 12 C boxes (Critical)        _____ points

Total of all 12 S boxes (Searching)       _____ points

Total of all 12 A boxes (Advising)        _____ points
                                          _____
                                  TOTAL    120  points
```

If your scores fall short of the 120 point total, follow this procedure for checking your totals:

- Look over each set of four boxes to see that the four ratings you entered (4, 3, 2, 1) add up to 10 points on each of the 12 episodes.
- Add up your 12 E ratings, placing an X over each E as you do so. Do the same with the other three letters in turn (C, S, A), until all 48 letters have an X on top of them, indicating that you've counted every rating.

The pages that follow will help you to interpret the implications of the four scores that you just entered in the tally box.

Interpreting Your Response Style

How are you likely to respond when someone speaks to you? What do you say? And what can you learn about the way you view others and relate to them? An analysis of your responses provides insights into your communication style and its impact on others.

The self-assessment you just completed yields four scores that indicate the degree to which you tend to respond with empathy (E), criticism (C), searching questions (S), or advice (A). These are the most common response modes in interpersonal communications. Let's look at each.

The Empathic Response E
The empathic response shows understanding—an attempt to put yourself in the other person's shoes. Whereas sympathy is a judgmental response of pity and often emotional, empathy is nonjudgmental ("I want to understand your position"). It is a rational, unemotional response.

The Critical Response C
The critical response shows disapproval—an attempt to let the other person know that you aren't satisfied or that you'd have handled things differently. Sometimes the intent is to be constructive and to improve things. However, the effect is often destructive, and Mark Twain once observed that there is no such thing as "constructive criticism," it's a contradiction in terms. Most people find that the critical response is their lowest score.

The Searching Response S
The searching response is an attempt to get additional information before acting. A high score here reflects that you ask questions frequently and recognize a need to find out more so that you can respond appropriately. An inquiring mind and a desire to understand people more fully are among your assets. This is usually one of the two higher scores of most people.

The Advising Response A
The advising response reflects a desire to help others by telling them what they should do. Although the intent may be supportive, the effect is not. The other party may not welcome the advice; they may take it as criticism or an insult or an attempt on your part to show that you have the answer. Moreover, your advice may over time make the other party dependent on you and keep them from working things out for themselves. Even when people ask for advice, they often want an understanding listener rather than an advisor.

Interpreting Your Scores

The Four Ego States

Your responses can be viewed on a grid that shows four life positions. This grid is shown in Figure 2.2. It is formed by two axes that intersect in the middle of the grid: I'm OK—I'm not OK, and You're OK—You're not OK. The four quadrants formed by these axes are labeled, using the language of transactional analysis (TA):

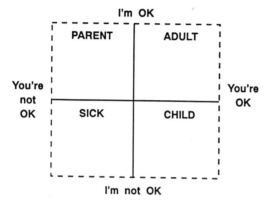

Figure 2.2

- Parent: I'm OK, You're not OK
- Adult: I'm OK, You're OK
- Child: You're OK, I'm not OK
- Sick: I'm not OK, You're not OK.

This first example ilustrates one type of parent: the judgmental parent. The parent is OK and the child not OK. "When are you going to learn to put your clothes away and tidy up your room? You ran off to the school bus today and left your room a wreck. You never allow enough time to clean up—I always have to pick up after you." It is often characterized by phrases like you should, you mustn't, you always, you never, why don't you ever, or I don't know when you're ever going to. Take a moment to enter the word *judgmental* in the PARENT block on the grid.

Being the parent is a state of mind; it consists of treating the other person like a child. It can occur in anyone, regardless of age. The following is an example of the judgmental parent as it might occur on the job. The speaker is a supervisor talking to an employee: "Pat, you didn't give me your time card last Friday. All the others gave me theirs. You know that I can't turn the departmental recap in until I have everyone's cards. Is there something I should know as to why you failed to turn your card in on time again?"

The other type of parent is the nurturing parent. It is characterized by a desire to help to the point of protecting, mollycoddling, or rescuing.

Take a moment to enter the word *nurturing* in the PARENT block on the grid under the word *judgmental*.

Let's convert the prior judgmental responses into nurturing ones: "I know you were running late today and almost missed the school bus. So I put your clothes away and tidied up your room. I'd suggest that you allow more time—maybe get up 10 minutes earlier. You might also want to lay out the clothes you want to wear the night before, to save you time in the morning."

And at work: "Pat, I see you're working on last Friday's time card. Look, it's after 5:00 and you coach the Little League tonight. Why don't you let me fill it out for you? Just sign it and run along—the kids are waiting. Don't worry about it. I'll take care of everything."

Parent-to-Child Responses

Notice that in our four examples, the parent put the other person in the child role. Whether or not they deserved it is irrelevant at this point. When you show that you are OK by judging or nurturing another person, they are automatically put into a not-OK state—that is, the child role.

Draw a diagonal line between the PARENT and CHILD quadrants on the diagram to reflect the parent-to-child interaction. Label this line *dependent*, because judgmental or nurturing comments place the other person in a dependency relationship; the child is dependent on the parent. There are times when others truly depend on us in a childlike (Not OK) manner; there are other times when people are themselves OK, yet we may be putting them into the child role with our parentlike treatment of them.

Adult-to-Adult Responses

The upper right quadrant is the adult response (I'm OK, You're OK). When you respond in an adult manner, you treat the other person as a fellow adult—with respect, trust, and commitment to a win-win transaction.

A moment ago you added a diagonal line to the grid and labeled it dependent. Adult-to-adult relations are interdependent: we need one another. Enter the word *adult* under the printed word *adult* and connect the two with a vertical line that you can label *interdependent* to reflect the nature of the adult-to-adult transaction.

Suppose I am your manager. If we have an adult-to-adult relationship, I do not see you as a subordinate. Your feelings are just as important to you as mine are to me. Your needs are just as pressing as are mine. Your perceptions of a situation are just as valid as mine. So I'd better hear you out and you'd better hear me out. And we'd better both work toward a win-win outcome, with which we're both satisfied (in contrast with the win-lose outcome that is typical of parent-to-child transactions).

The only way you are my subordinate and I am your superior is on an organization chart. But in a matrix organization or one in which teams are used to get things done, the formal organization chart (pyramidal, multilayered) disappears, and teams begin to replace or cut across hierarchies (see Figure 2.3).

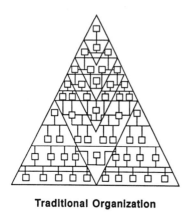

Traditional Organization **Matrix Organization**
Figure 2.3

Child-to-Parent Responses

A word about the CHILD quadrant. If we want to treat others as adults, they must be willing and able to function in the ADULT quadrant. However, not everybody wants to, or can. Consider Lee, an employee who comes to you and says:

"I know you showed me yesterday how this should be done, but I thought I'd better check with you to see if I'm doing it right—the way you told me. I wouldn't want to mess up and make you or the big boss mad."

You reflect on all the time you spent with Lee yesterday, going through the assignment in detail and getting feedback that indicated a good level of comfort and understanding. And here Lee is again, camping on your doorstep and looking for reassurance and approval. Lee is the child in this example, looking to you for nurture or judgment.

The child looks for both. When a Lee comes to you and says: "I don't know if I'm doing this the way you wanted. I may have messed up." You may try to respond as an adult: "Well, where are you having doubts? Can you pinpoint your uncertainty?" But suppose Lee remains childlike: "I just want to know if I'm doing it in a way that will make you happy." So you now look over Lee's work and are likely to give a parent response, either nurturing Lee (You're doing fine, Lee.) or becoming judgmental (You haven't got it quite right, Lee. Let me show you.)

Summary

- A parent comment is calculated to elicit a child response. Similarly, a child comment is intended to elicit a parent response.
- You can respond to a parent or child comment in an adult manner.

Sometimes it will influence the other person to respond in the adult role; at other times the transaction will remain crossed, or unbalanced.
- An adult comment usually elicits an adult response unless the respondent is already thinking parent or child thoughts.
- In an organization in which employees are interdependent, adult-to-adult transactions are the norm. In contrast, bureaucratic, hierarchical organizations tend to foster parent-to-child relationships and transactions.
- An interaction that was initiated on a parent or child basis can often be converted to an adult-to-adult basis by responding as an adult. These are the norm in an empowered organization. In contrast, bureaucratic, hierarchical organizations typically foster parent-to-child relationships and transactions.
- Sometimes the other party is definitely not OK (i.e., child or sick), in which case a parent response may be most appropriate.

What Is Your Predominant Style?

Do your interactions with others tend to be parent-to-child? Or are they mainly adult-to-adult? To what degree are you empathic (E), critical (C), searching (S), and advising (A)? Now that we've defined and illustrated these terms, let's look at your communication style, and then at your management style.

The assessment you just completed measured your responses in the upper two quadrants: PARENT and ADULT. It did not measure the degree to which your responses might be CHILD or SICK. However, most people who are successful in their jobs communicate primarily in the upper quadrants—the I'm OK half of the model we looked at earlier.

Look now at the four scores on page 14 (the numbers that added up to 120). As you reflect on the meaning of E, C, S, and A, it is clear you have probably realized that the critical and advising responses are parent in nature (judgmental and nurturing, respectively), while the empathic and searching responses are adult in nature.

Add your C and A scores to get your parent score: _____ .
Add your E and S scores to get your adult score: _____

A comparison of these two numbers shows the degree to which your interactions with others tend to be parent-to-child or adult-to-adult.

Communication Style and Management Style

We've been examining your E, C, S, and A responses as a clue to how you communicate. Now let's relate this to management style (i.e., leadership style, selling style, and instructional style).

In 1960, Dr. Douglas McGregor outlined his Theory X and Theory Y, two ways of managing, in *The Human Side of Enterprise* (published by McGraw-Hill, Inc). The way we deal with others, McGregor explained, is based on our assumptions about them. Theory X managers assume that their people are not performing at the levels they should be, either because they are incompetent or lazy (judgmental, Hard X) or because they're new or just kids (nurturing, Soft X). In contrast, Theory Y managers assume that their people are responsible adults, capable of growth and high levels of achievement.

The Pygmalion effect is well known. There's a self-fulfilling prophecy at work whenever we make assumptions about people: you get what you expect. If you treat your employees (customers or students) in a parent-to-child manner based on Theory X assumptions, they will perform below the level they are capable of. But if you employ Theory Y assumptions and treat them in an adult-to-adult manner, they will perform at their best.

Self-Quiz on Your Response Style

1. Were there any surprises as you examined your E, C, S, and A scores? Or do you feel they portray your communication style fairly accurately?

2. Who are the major persons at work to whom you relate on a parent-to-child basis? On an adult-to-adult basis?

3. Which of these persons would you like to work with in modifying the way you relate? How might this be done?

4. What is your reaction to the ratio of your Theory X style (C + A) to your Theory Y style (S + E)? What are the key influences in your life that have given you this ratio?

5. What forces, influences, or actions are at work in your organization that are helping to move the culture toward empowerment and adult-to-adult relationships?

6. What forces are hindering the move toward empowerment and serving to perpetuate parent-to-child relationships?

7. Do you think it is possible or appropriate to have the organization arrive at a 100% adult-to-adult basis of relationships at some future time? Explain.

8. What are the implications of your answers to these questions on a personal basis? On an organizational basis? What actions should be taken?

3 Changing The Corporate Culture

For empowerment to work, organizations must find new models for managing and new ways of viewing the world (as described in Peter Senge's book, *The Fifth Discipline*). A paradigm shift is needed. Unlike the chicken and egg analogy (one of them must have come first), empowerment and the paradigm shift occur simultaneously.

Most organizations have spent years generating reams of policy and procedures, rules and regulations, and rewards and punishments to control employees and keep them in their places as loyal, obedient, and disempowered children. Within the past decade, however, many of these organizations have attempted to invert the pyramid and develop bottoms-up management in which customers and employees are driving the company. That's some paradigm shift!

Recently the president of Malaysian Airlines System (MAS) told me that he cannot fly a plane, ticket a passenger, process cargo, confirm a reservation, or do any of the jobs of the 50 persons required to meet the needs of a passenger. "My job is to enable them to do their jobs better. I must serve MAS employees in ways that help them to serve customers with excellence."

Upon completing chapter 3, you should be able to:

- Identify at least five factors or trends of the 20th century that account for the current paradigm shift (i.e., from parent-to-child to adult-to-adult).
- Describe at least six differences in the assumptions or beliefs found in Theory X and Theory Y organizations.
- Identify the four major groupings of managerial competencies, indicating how each relates to task-oriented and people-oriented behavior.

- Illustrate by example the relationship between organizational climate and culture and the ways in which managers make use of their competencies.
- List at least 8 of the 12 competencies that are important to a leader's effectiveness.
- Select any two of the competencies to illustrate by example how a Theory X and a Theory Y manager might apply these competencies at work.
- Analyze your own organization's behavior on each of the 12 competencies determining the degree to which it is parent-to-child (X) and adult-to-adult (Y) on each.
- Indicate what action might be taken on each competency that accelerates the paradigm shift toward empowerment and effective teamwork.

Theory X has been the predominant way of doing business throughout recorded history. At the turn of the last century, U.S. companies were almost 100% Theory X, and parent-child relationships prevailed in the home, church, school, and place of work.

Soft work (e.g., cottage industries and mom and pop businesses) produced the Soft X style, known as benevolent paternalism. Hard work (e.g., foundries, mining, steel, automotive, or railroads) produced the Hard X style, and the employees reacted by forming unions to protect themselves against the abuses of ownership and their hired managers (see Figure 3.1)

I'm OK—You're not OK Theory X	I'm OK—You're OK Theory Y
Parent—based on win-lose outcome	Adult—based on win-win outcome
Hard X: Judgmental; Critical responses; Autocratic.	Mutual respect; team work; interdependence.
Soft X: Nurturing: Advising responses; Benevolent paternalism.	Manager is coach, not boss; employees manage themselves.

Figure 3.1

Parent-to-child relationships predominated in the early 1900s and, for that matter, well into the century for many reasons:

- The work force was largely immigrant. Many employees didn't know the language (the ultimate Not OK) and expected to be treated as children.
- Many firms actually employed children, often in unsafe environments, which led to legislation and a rigid code of what employees can and can't do.

- Many individuals used all their own money and even went into debt to start their businesses. This greater stake in the success of the business led many to assume the judgmental parent role.
- The Victorian Era (1840s to 1900s) fostered strong parent-to-child relationships in the home, church, school, and workplace.
- The emerging technology of the industrial revolution (i.e., electricity and complex machinery) left most employees Not OK and dependent on their overseers.
- Education had created a caste system in the industrialized world: managers were educated, most workers were not.

Some of these conditions prevailed throughout the first half of the century. The impact of two World Wars helped to perpetuate the Theory X style of management. Indeed, it is only within recent years (i.e., the 1960s through the 1980s) that a number of trends and social movements emerged and contributed to moving the U.S. rapidly into a Theory Y method of managing affairs at home and at work. Some of these included:

- Equal rights for women, minorities, and physically and mentally challenged individuals (everyone is OK).
- Foreign competition, technology, and the pace of change require a team approach to business.
- Today's employees are the best educated in all of recorded history.
- Children mature earlier and demand adult status earlier.
- In business, risk is shared among many stakeholders and stockholders.
- Employees want a say in how they can work most productively.

The following two-column table presents a comparison of Theory X and Theory Y assumptions. As Douglas McGregor explained, these assumptions prompt us to behave in a parent-child manner toward some people and in an adult-adult manner toward others.

The culture of an organization can be described with many other terms: formal versus informal, reactive versus proactive, and status quo versus risk-taking. However, because the culture of an organization is influenced most directly by the style of its employees at all levels and the nature of their relationships, we focus on their interactions with others. McGregor named the two general styles of interaction X and Y. Other pairs of teams include boss-coach, autocratic-democratic, and our own tormentor-mentor. We prefer parent-child and adult-adult, because they seem to be readily understood and make it easier for us to catch ourselves in the act of treating someone else as a child by being overly judgmental or nurturing. Are they facilitating or interfering with the work of others? Are they enhancing or jeopardizing quality?

During the 1980s, a number of leading corporations conducted studies

Two Sets of Assumptions about People

	Theory X	Theory Y
Human Nature	People are naturally passive; they prefer to do nothing. People remain children grown larger; they are naturally dependent on others to lead and to reward or punish them. People have little concern beyond their immediate, material interests. People naturally resist change; they prefer the security of the status quo and must be motivated by external factors.	People are naturally active; they set goals and enjoy striving. People normally mature beyond childhood; they aspire to independence, self-fulfillment, and responsibility. People seek to give meaning to their lives by identifying with nations, communities, churches, unions, companies, and causes. People naturally tire of routine and enjoy new experiences and opportunities for growth.
Training and Development	People need to be told, shown, and trained in proper methods of work. People need specific instruction on what to do and how to do it. Larger policy issues do not concern them. People are shaped by heredity, childhood, and youth; as adults they remain static; old dogs don't learn new tricks.	People who understand and care about what they are doing can devise and improve their own methods of doing work. People need to see the big picture and to know the why behind their work. They constantly grow, and it is never too late to learn; they enjoy learning and increasing their knowledge and skills.
Supervision and Leadership	People expect and depend on direction from above; they do not want to think for themselves. People need supervisors who will watch them closely, praise their good work, and reprimand errors.	People close to the situation see and feel what is needed and are capable of self-direction. People need to be respected and treated as capable of assuming responsibility and self-correction.
Motivation and Rewards	Work itself isn't satisfying; people need money and status rewards to get them to work. The main force keeping people productive in their work is fear of being demoted or fired. People need to be inspired, pushed, or driven.	Work offers many satisfactions: pride in achievement, social contacts, new challenges, and growth. The main force keeping people productive in their work is a desire to achieve their personal and social goals. People need to be released, given an area of freedom.
Work and Jobs	Jobs come first; people are selected, trained, and fitted to meet the needs of the job. People are naturally compartmentalized; work demands are entirely different from leisure activities.	People come first; workers seek self-realization; and jobs must be designed, modified, and fitted to people. People are naturally integrated; when work and play are too sharply separated, both suffer.

to identify the competencies that made a significant difference in the performance of managers. High-performing managers were found to display greater proficiency in certain competencies. These competencies fall into two major areas of activity: task and people.

These two major areas are divided further. The task side of your job divides into administrative and cognitive, and the people side divides into communication and supervisory. These four, in turn, have major competencies under each, as shown in Figure 3.2.

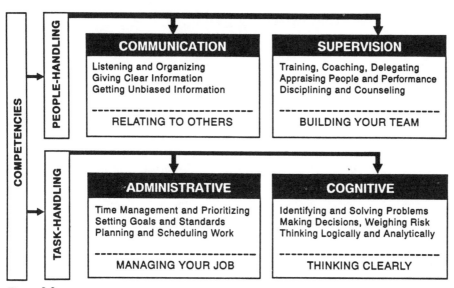

Figure 3.2

Our interest in this taxonomy of competencies is quite simple: managers whose preferred style is parent-to-child will apply each competency quite differently from managers who favor adult-to-adult relationships. Because everyone is a manager in the empowered organization, we can make conclusions about the behavior of the entire work force. The table on the next four pages compares the two styles, competency by competency. The first two deal with the task side of your job (i.e., administrative and cognitive competencies), and the final two pages show the people side (i.e., communication and supervisory competencies).

The Administrative Competencies
(as applied by two styles of managers)

	Parent-to-Child (Theory X)	Adult-to-Adult (Theory Y)
Time Management and Prioritizing	Wants to see people keeping busy all the time—activity oriented.	Believes there should be quiet times and moments for reflecting and planning—results oriented.
	Manages the time of others, who can't be expected to know the priorities.	Trusts people to manage their own time and does not second-guess them on priorities.
	Believes everything must get done sooner or later, so keep working.	Believes getting everything done is not as important as getting the right things done.
	Expects people to be available whenever they are needed; putting in time is of prime importance.	Recognizes that people have many priorities and aren't always available; achieving results is more important than putting in time.
Setting Goals and Standards	Assigns tasks and activities, often without explaining goals.	Assigns goals and standards, explains what the results should look like and why.
	Tells employees the details of how a goal or standard should be met.	Lets employees work out the details of how a goal or standard should be met.
	Believes that employees don't need or want to know goals and standards and that they are happy as long as they are busy.	Believes that employees have a critical stake in knowing the goals and standards and that tracking performance toward them is a key source of motivation.
	Views goal setting as a threatening activity and therefore sets personal goals that are unrealistically high or low.	Views goals setting as a growth and development activity and therefore sets personal goals that are challenging but achievable.
Planning and Scheduling	Feels that there's no time to plan or schedule, and that because things never go according to plan anyway, there is no need to bother.	Feels that planning, scheduling, and controlling are part of every job; we must take time to make time.
	Sees activity as productive (visible output) and may distrust planning as a poor substitute for working.	Sees planning as working. Effective planning should enable people to work smarter rather than harder.
	Views planning and scheduling as management responsibilities, because employees (children) can't be expected to know how to handle it.	Views planning and scheduling as an important part of any task or assignment and thus the responsibility of everyone. Managers and employees must confer on how to handle it.

The Cognitive Competencies
(as applied by two styles of managers)

	Parent-to-Child (Theory X)	Adult-to-Adult (Theory Y)
Identifying and Solving Problems	Believes that management has the responsibility and superior experience to solve problems, and employees should not attempt to do it themselves.	Believes that the employees closest to the problems are in the best position to solve them, given proper training and coaching.
	Sees empowerment as a threat to quality as unprepared employees attempt to solve problems themselves.	Sees empowerment as a means of placing responsibility with teams and work groups, where it belongs.
	May at times be more interested in assigning blame than in resolving problems.	Avoids blaming employees, prefers to view problems as opportunities for learning—live case studies.
	Sees problems as a curse or mistake on someone's part.	Sees problems as a natural part of any endeavor.
Making Decisions, Weighing Risk	Believes it is the role of a manager to make decisions and the role of employees to put these decisions into action.	Believes many decisions can and should be made by employees. Managers and employees should work out in advance the types of decisions each is responsible for.
	Tends to base decisions on subjective factors and gut feelings. The process is sometimes emotional.	Tends to base decisions on objective data. Weighs the alternatives on different factors, sometimes with a decision matrix. Takes a rational, unemotional approach.
	Views the ability to make decisions as a major source of power. To delegate or share it means a loss of personal power or influence.	Views empowerment as more effectiveness for everyone. Employees will be more committed to the successful outcome of decisions that they researched and made.
Thinking Clearly and Analytically	Tends to oversimplify and to polarize issues as black and white.	Tends to see many shades of gray when analyzing people and situations.
	Often unaware of personal bias or of alternative ways of viewing things.	Solicits opinions and viewpoints of others to get a broader perception of things.
	May lead with the heart and follow with the head.	Keeps facts and feelings separate, treating reason and emotion with equal respect.
	Jumps to premature conclusions, does not look for evidence or assign weight, and is easily victimized by faulty logic.	Takes time to weigh evidence, explore alternatives, test assumptions, and evaluate the soundness of the input (premises) and output (conclusions).

The Communication Competencies
(as applied by two styles of managers)

	Parent-to-Child (Theory X)	Adult-to-Adult (Theory Y)
Listening and Organizing	May not spot gaps or inconsistencies in what others are saying.	Probes to confirm understanding and get closure.
	Believes that people say what they mean and mean what they say.	Believes that people aren't always sure what they want to say.
	Fails to summarize or confirm understanding. Assumes that message clarity is the speaker's responsibility.	Confirms and seeks closure with summary: Let me see if I understand what you've been saying. You feel that ...
	Is often better at listening for facts and content than for feelings and intent.	Pays as much attention to the speaker's **Intent** as to the message **content**; works to answer the question: Why are you telling me this?
Giving Clear Information	Believes that one person is the sender and the other is the receiver of information. Therefore, the ability to make an effective (commanding, one-way) presentation is the key to influencing others.	Believes that both parties have information to give and get, and that this is done via dialogue from the Greek words *dia* ("through") and *logos* ("logic"). Dialogue literally means working the meaning through two or more people.
	Believes that attitudes are hard to change but that it can be done by conveying the right information.	Believes that attitudes can be changed better by asking questions than by giving information—deductive (Socratic) discussion and dialogue rather than inductive lecture.
	Sees breakdowns in communication as the other person's fault: You didn't listen when I told you.	Sees communication as a two-way street. Both parties are responsible for making sure that understanding is complete.
Getting Unbiased Information	Believes employees, like children should be seen and not heard; does not probe for verification.	Believes that the speaker deserves full attention and a "clean slate" (no prior listener bias or assumptions of source credibility).
	Is often better at listening for factual information than for feelings and thoughts.	Probes for feelings (Why are you telling me this?) as well as for fact (What information are you conveying?)
	Uses directive questions that tend to bias the respondent into saying what is expedient (i.e., the reply is often guarded, incomplete, and phrased in acceptable terms).	Uses the full repertoire of questions (directive, nondirective, self-appraisal, probes) to get the full message (content and intent).

The Supervisory Competencies
(as applied by two styles of managers)

	Parent-to-Child (Theory X)	Adult-to-Adult (Theory Y)
Training, Coaching, and Delegating	Views the glass as half empty. There's so much that our people must learn and so little time to teach it (show and tell, inductive method).	Views the glass as half full. We can train our people by building on what they already know (Socratic, deductive method).
	Feels his or her role is to tell employees what they need to know to perform effectively.	Feels his or her role is to help employees learn by experience with hands-on activity in a low-risk, fail-safe environment.
	Thinks employees depend on the manager to share experience and knowledge.	Thinks employees are self-dependent as long as managers provide the needed resources (mentors, co-workers, instructors).
	Believes that training can and should be delegated to HRD people, who are the experts.	Believes that training of one's team is too important to be delegated (it can only be abdicated!).
	Sees the teacher's role as active and the learner's as a largely passive and submissive listener—who shouldn't interrupt or challenge.	Sees learner's role as active and teacher's role as an arranger of learning experiences—welcomes interruptions and challenges.
Appraising People and Performance	Gives little if any specific feedback. The judgmental manager (Hard X) is critical and hard to please, while the nurturing manager (Soft X) gives overall and general encouragement without pinpointing specific correct and incorrect behavior.	Gives regular feedback, both complimentary and corrective, so that both types are seen as normal and welcome. Such feedback is thus reinforcing (i.e., effective in shaping the desired behavior).
	Sometimes waits until annual appraisal to evaluate. Performance reviews contain surprises and may be emotional.	Gives regular feedback so that annual appraisals are surprise-free—a time for taking inventory, identifying trends, and planning future growth actions.
	Wants the employee to know how he or she stacks up in the eyes of a superior's expectations.	Wants the employee to appraise self and thus internalize the standards and the responsibility (self-management).
Disciplining and Counseling	Sees discipline as a negative action that must be taken to punish or make a point or get even.	Sees discipline as a constructive action that must be taken to restore behavior to desirable levels.
	Believes that it's the **person** that is unacceptable and must be corrected.	Believes that it's the **behavior** that is unacceptable and must be corrected.
	May avoid discipline in the hope that the problem or deviation will go away or get better on its own.	Sees the need to correct inappropriate behavior when it is first recognized, before it becomes habit and thus harder to correct.

Self-Quiz on Changing the Corporate Culture

1. List at least five factors or trends of the 20th century that help to explain the shift from parent-to-child to adult-to-adult relationships.

2. How do the assumptions (beliefs) of Theory X organizations differ from those of Theory Y organizations? See if you can describe at least six differences.

3. What are the four major groupings of managerial competencies? Which are task oriented? Which are people oriented?

4. Describe the relationship between your organization's climate or culture and the way in which managers make use of their competencies.

5. This chapter described twelve managerial competencies. List at least eight of them that you feel are important to a leader's effectiveness.

6. Select two competencies from your answer to question 5 and explain how a Theory X and Theory Y manager might apply these competencies at work.

7. Of the twelve competencies described in this chapter, which two or three bring out the strongest parent-child (Theory X) behavior in your managers? On which two or three do your managers show the strongest adult-adult (Theory Y) behavior?

8. On each competency on which you feel the organization's practices are more parent than adult, what actions might be taken to speed up the shift to Theory Y, empowerment, and teamwork?

9. What are some of the behaviors (i.e., practices, actions, or policies) in your organization that you can cite as examples of a Theory X (parent-to-child) culture?

10. What are some of the behaviors in your organization that exemplify a Theory Y (adult-to-adult) culture?

11. Consider the total number of interactions that take place throughout the organization, between and among all levels of employees and management. What percentage of these would you guess are conducted on a parent-to-child basis and on an adult-to-adult basis? Enter your guess in the middle row on Figure 3.3. Then estimate the same percentages for the organization the way it was 10 years ago. Then guess what the relative strength of X and Y might be 10 years from now.

	Theory X (Parent-to-Child)	Theory Y (Adult-to-Adult)
10 Years Ago	_____ %	_____ %
Today	_____ %	_____ %
10 Years From Now	_____ %	_____ %

Figure 3.3

12. In the Theory X column, what is the difference between your first two estimates (10 years ago versus today)? _____ . And what is the difference between your second two estimates (today versus 10 years from now)? _____ . Comparing these two numbers, is the rate of change accelerating or decelerating in your organization?

Discussion Leadership Skills

The best industrial relations
Involve two-way communications
Along whose lines, from foot to crown,
Ideas flow up and vetoes down.

Kenneth Boulding
University of Michigan, 1950s

Like the flow of blood in our bodies, the free flow of information is essential to the health of an organization. A century ago the flow was mainly downward, from the owners to the workers. A half-century later the introduction of suggestion systems and employee attitude surveys made the flow a two-way affair. But the tracks still ran vertically on the organization chart.

Today, the tracks run horizontally as well as vertically. Facts and feelings are flowing freely between team members, between teams, between line and staff functions, and between organizations that want to learn from one another's best practices (i.e., benchmarking).

We are reminded of the seven blind Hindu Indians trying to understand what an elephant looks like. One grasps the tail: "Tis like a rope!" he exclaims. Another feels a leg: "Tis like a tree trunk!" Another feels the trunk: "Tis like a hose!" No one has the entire picture, and the seven will never understand unless a lot of sharing of information takes place.

Like the blind Hindus, we must share our perceptions and our ideas if TQM employee involvement and participative management are to succeed. Discussion is the means by which facts and feelings are shared. You've participated in thousands of discussions. What percentage of them were successful? And what criteria would you use to require their success?

Because group dynamics and discussion leadership skills are so integral a part of empowerment, we've devoted chapters 4 through 6 to the tools and techniques that you should find helpful. Upon completing chapter 4, you should be able to:

- Describe the roles that you might fill as a discussion leader, and give an example of the type of meeting that might call for each role.
- State the three major factors that should influence your discussion leadership style.
- Select from a list of 36 guidelines the ones that apply and are relevant to the types of discussion you are responsible for conducting.
- Identify at least six guidelines that you have not applied in the past but plan to apply in the future.
- Write a reminder list of your guidelines (e.g., on a file card) that you can have in front of you when you next lead a discussion.
- Repeat the action just described with a new reminder list after the initial guidelines you selected have become a natural part of your facilitation skills repertoire.

The process of discussion is a cornerstone of any democratic organization, from the family to the company to society and the country. The reasons are many and well known: getting all sides heard (pro and con), increasing the commitment and buy-in of all parties, uncovering and dealing with lesser known but highly relevant facts and opinions, educating all parties to the issues, and so on.

When applied in the workplace, discussion enables participants to think things through for themselves, to reason, to weigh alternatives, and to learn to accept perspectives and perceptions that are different from their own. This is why analysis and discussion are essential to the success of any group-based form of experiential learning: role playing, case method, games and simulations, and assessments.

The techniques and leadership style you select in your role as discussion leader depend on three major factors: the purpose of the meeting (objectives), the experience level of participants and their willingness to share (group input), and the levels of rank and status that are present (balance of power).

Figure 4.1 shows how your style can spread across a wide continuum,

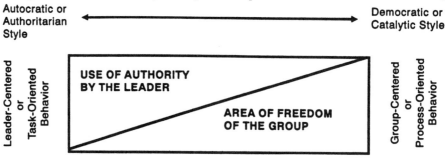

Figure 4.1

ranging from strong input and control on your part (e.g., teaching a group of new hires an unfamiliar procedure) to moderating and recording the strong input of participants (e.g., leading a self-directed team in problem solving).

What style you display depends on how you use the power you hold as discussion leader. Are you asking questions and making observations in a way that helps participants work things out for themselves? Or do you expect to control the group and to get them to accept your conclusions?

There's a place for each type of leadership. The military commander who invites discussion and questions following a battlefield briefing is at the left end of our diagram. So are the company's chief executives inviting discussion from the floor at the annual stockholder's meeting. In contrast, an outside consultant running a focus group to elicit employee opinion will operate at the right end of the diagram. And an instructor conducting a management development program will probably operate somewhere in the middle.

As discussion leader, you must maintain control of the interaction and dynamics, doing everything within your power to see that the objectives are met. The way in which you do this and the nature of the objectives determine where your leadership style falls on the continuum shown in our diagram.

Roles and Responsibilities

The pages that follow contain 36 guidelines for fulfilling your responsibility as a discussion leader. You must decide how relevant each is to your role and style, which again depends on the purpose, nature of the group, and distribution of power. As you read the list, you might want to circle the suggestions that apply to the kinds of sessions you lead. The guidelines are not listed in any particular order.

1. Focus Discussion

Participants have many different opinions, observations, needs, and agendas. This means that discussion will ramble, with comments scattered in many directions. There's a difference between orderly discussion and a bull session, and it's your job to make that difference. You can do this in an autocratic manner: "Harry, that's not part of our agenda (mission, objective)." Or you can be a catalyst: "Harry, I'm having trouble relating your comment to our objectives. Can you help me out?"

2. Clarify Objectives

At the start of a discussion or shortly thereafter, it's appropriate to get the participants' agreement on objectives and how the group will know that

From Managing to Empowering

they've been met. Again, whether you dictate the objectives or help the group formulate them depends on your purpose.

3. Budget Time

Although it's very easy to lose control of the time, you have a responsibility to end the discussion by a reasonable time that should be agreed to in advance. This enables you to say things like, "We've spent almost 10 minutes on this item. Do you think we can wind it up and move on in another 2 to 3 minutes, or do you need more time?"

4. Keep Moving

Although you want to focus on one issue at a time, you will often become stalled when two or more participants begin arguing a point between themselves and everyone else becomes a spectator. It might be necessary to say something like: "I'd love to let you continue, but it's clear that we're not going to resolve your differences in the next two minutes. So let me suggest that we move on to consider the next topic."

5. Ensure Coverage

You have prepared in advance and know what key points or issues should be covered during the discussion. If the group begins to reach closure or come to premature conclusions without addressing these issues, you should bring them up: "Did I hear anyone mention the issue of . . . ?" Or perhaps, "You know, another aspect of the situation that occurs to me is the fact that . . . ."

6. Highlight Inconsistencies

Sometimes participants will agree with a point of view and then support a conflicting view 10 minutes later. Didn't they see the conflict? Or did you see a conflict that isn't there? It's your job to challenge the group: "I'm confused. Earlier I heard you agree with . . . and now I'm hearing . . . . Aren't these two viewpoints inconsistent? Or is it possible for the two to exist without conflict?"

7. Save Face

Hidden agendas, personality differences, and mounting frustration are a few of the reasons a group or an individual may attack a participant and cause loss of face. A basic principle is to preserve the group's integrity and not allow anyone to be put down. You might need to interrupt such behavior: "Wait a minute. Before we throw any more rocks at Joanne, I'd like to share my view of the situation."

8. Record Milestones

A good way to keep the group moving and focused is to record any major decisions, actions, and points of agreement that the group has reached. By summarizing in 6 to 12 words on the flipchart, you can close the curtain on one issue and move on to the next one. In addition, if you've agreed on a game plan or agenda for budgeting your time, it's often useful to record this on a flipchart sheet for all to see. Then draw a line through each item as you complete it. (The following guideline illustrates a typical game plan.)

9. Plan the Phases

Discussion usually flows in a pattern. Both decision-making and problem-solving discussions follow certain processes or phases. Here is an all-purpose list of five phases of discussion:

1. What is the situation? (description of problem or opportunity)
2. How do we know? (evidence and its relevance or credibility)
3. What do we want to accomplish? (objectives)
4. How will we know we've arrived? (criteria of acceptability)
5. How will we implement? (recommendations, actions, and plan)

10. Deal with Problems

Disruptive behavior from one or more participants can keep the group from accomplishing your objectives. Your responsibility to the group is to control disruptive participants who dominate, challenge, refuse to accept, withdraw, or form cliques. Don't let these people poison the open, positive climate you've worked to build. You might deal with negative Bob with: "Okay, Bob, you've given us several reasons for not installing the new system. There are two sides to every issue, so let's spend a few minutes on the benefits. Who can give us some?"

11. Facilitate, Don't Dominate

You bring a wealth of personal experience to the group. It's easy, therefore, to share these with the group. However, don't let them get in the way of your primary role, which is to draw out the group members. Let them share experiences that help to illustrate a point. Or, if you are drawing on a personal example, you might depersonalize by saying, "One of our employees had an experience that . . . "

12. Establish Ground Rules

For certain groups or types of discussion, you may want to set some guidelines at the start to make the discussion as smooth as possible. Here are a few examples:

- Don't interrupt—hear the other person out.
- Put group goals above personal agendas.
- Participate—share your ideas and reactions with others.
- Identify assumptions—ask for evidence, facts, or support.
- One person speaks at a time.
- Work toward agreement by consensus, not majority vote.

13. Get Full Participation
Pareto's 80-20 rule applies to group interaction: 80% of your contributions and discussion come from 20% of the participants. Forming subgroups of 3 to 4 persons and giving them a few minutes to discuss an issue and make recommendations can help get this 20% up to 100%. Asking each person to write down at least three ideas for the discussion or posing a question and having participants answer to their neighbor, working in pairs, can also help. The success of your session depends on getting as much participation as you can.

14. Withhold Personal Opinion
Your participants have had years of parent-child relationships with the person up front—that is, the teacher or boss. They've been conditioned to expect answers, directions, solutions, and decisions from the authority figures in their lives. It's common to hear someone say, "Well, what do you think we should do? You've been down this road before." It's best to withhold your own contribution (unless it's factual input that they need regarding policy or rules) until you've gotten all you can from the group. Your mission is to facilitate their thinking, not to share your own.

15. Set a Positive Climate
The world of work is filled with negatives: "It will never work, We tried that once," or "Management doesn't want us to." An effective discussion requires a positive climate that is supportive and accepting. You might suggest that your session is a laboratory in which participants are free to try out new ideas, express opinions, and share experience without fear of being rejected or embarrassed.

16. Use Non-Directive Questions
When you want to open discussion and elicit full contribution, use nondirective (open-ended) questions: "How do you feel about this policy? What effects is it likely to have? What do you think the company should do to implement it?" Using nondirective questions is like fishing with a net . . . you want to cast it wide and catch everything that's out there.

17. Use Directive Questions
When you want to reach closure, summarize, get agreement on a point, or elicit a specific answer, use directive (structured) questions that lead to a particular response: "Are we in agreement, then, that the policy has some shortcomings but should probably be implemented? Do you want to spend more time on this issue, or should we move ahead?"

18. Take Inventory
When leading a lengthy discussion (e.g., more than half an hour), you might want to set some checkpoints at which you can stop and take inventory: "Now, let's take a moment to see what we've accomplished so far." This

should include points you've agreed to, points you agreed to disagree about, and issues that you haven't addressed yet.

19. Share the Responsibility

In some types of meetings, you might want to share the responsibility of leading the group. Here are five roles that might be assigned to different members of the group:

- Recorder at flip chart. Writing key ideas and contributions.
- Time keeper. Reminding the group of the agenda and checkpoints.
- Monitor. Pointing out (with a STOP sign) digressions, irrelevancies, off limits (union contract issues), or nonproductive negatives.
- Follow-up recorder. Preparing minutes of meeting on decisions reached and who will do what before next meeting.
- Subject matter expert. Persons who are present because of their technical or professional expertise.

20. Summarize, Give Closure

End your discussion with a summary statement that gives closure to what has been accomplished. If you're leading a meeting, you can use the agenda or the flipchart notes as your outline. If you're facilitating a training session, you can refer to the objectives and recount the actions that were taken to meet these objectives. If you have participants who can summarize, involve them in the final wrap-up: "First of all, we tackled the issue of arrival time. Ken, perhaps you can summarize the conclusions we came to."

21. Allow Enough Time

Although this guideline might seem to conflict with guideline 3: Budget Time, participants do need time to question, challenge, and react with alternatives—in short, to buy in to new ideas. If agreement is reached before this happens (perhaps because the clock is running out), doubts, frustration, and tension will follow after the meeting and will undermine the implementation of any decisions and actions that were agreed to in haste.

22. Elicit Pros and Cons

Both positive and negative reactions are important to the successful outcome of a discussion. According to studies at Harvard, the ideal balance is twice as many positive as negative. You may get a lot of negatives at the start. Record them, but then show that for each negative there's a paired positive. To achieve the ideal balance, ask, "Now, are there any other positive benefits you can think of besides the ones that are the twins of our original negative list?"

23. Know the Players

A sports team has players with different skills appropriate to the positions they fill. Similarly, the participants in a discussion can be counted on to fill different positions. Their behavior is predictable, based on the roles they've filled in prior meetings. For example, some are good initiators of ideas, some are supporters, some are challengers, and some will keep the group on target by restating the objectives. Learn your players and know who can be counted on to deliver the skills needed at different points during the discussion.

24. Control Group Size

You may not be able to influence the size of your group other than to divide it into working subgroups. When the group has more than 10 participants, it's usually worthwhile to look for assignments or activities that enable you to create subgroups.

25. Insulate Difficult Members

A group of five to seven participants can usually absorb a difficult member (e.g., too negative, talkative, opinionated, or insensitive). The best strategy might be to surround such a person with high-participation members and thereby insulate the group from the difficult member. In addition, by breaking into subgroup activities, the members of a subgroup are more likely to deal with a difficult member, which no one is likely to attempt in the full group (or, if they do, you may have an even more difficult situation on your hands!).

26. Balance the Participation Levels

Some members are high-participation types who will speak out in any size group on any issue. Others maintain an invisible profile at the low-participation end of the continuum. A range of these types is best. Groups made up of only the high participators suffer from too much competition, while having all low participants produces less creativity and fewer ideas.

27. Balance the Task-People Needs

Discussion leadership requires a balance between task needs (e.g., meet the objectives, cover the agenda, and agree on actions) and people needs (e.g., express feelings, strengthen relationships, and socialize). Some organizations will use two leaders to conduct sessions; for example: a subject matter expert with a facilitator in training programs, or a content leader with a process leader on self-directed work teams.

28. Start with Facts and Evidence

Even when the facts and evidence are familiar to most participants, your discussion should start by reviewing them. This provides a uniform foundation for any action the group takes, and it helps you to avoid the tendency of participants to begin with opinions and specific suggestions.

"Well, if you ask me, what we should do is.... I don't agree. What the company should have done is..., and because we didn't do that, now we've got...." You can avoid such a start by pooling the facts and their relevance from the members of your group.

29. Move from Words to Experience
Often a disagreement or argument can be resolved by getting participants to share specific ideas and avoid general statements. In other words, the premises or conclusions are faulty, but we need to know the events or "referents" that produced them. Often participants do not draw each other out far enough to realize that they are thinking of different experiences with which both could readily agree but drawing generalizations and using words with which they disagree.

30. Retreat and Regroup
A famous general once said, "He who lives to run away will live to fight another day." When emotions begin to mount or when negative comments or disagreements begin to threaten the climate of the group, retreat to earlier ground. Here's one way of doing this: "Let me interrupt at this point, because I feel that we may have lost sight of some of the facts we reviewed earlier and the agreement we reached regarding our objectives. We said that...."

31. Keep It Simple
Sometimes a discussion leader with a background in the behavioral sciences will want to share a concept, cite a theory, quote a historical precedent or anecdote, or summarize what has just happened in the group by using abstractions, generalizations, and a multisyllable vocabulary that is more appropriate to a journal article than a discussion. Keep it simple. Avoid comments like this: Perhaps we're in a Catch 22 situation here, a bit like Sisyphus in Greek mythology. We may be allowing peripheral issues to obfuscate the obvious and cause our regression. Instead, use one-syllable words and avoid references that are unfamiliar. Translation: "We seem to be sliding backwards here. Side issues may be clouding our view and pushing us off the main track, which is to ... "

32. Create a Parking Lot
From time to time, participants will bring up an issue that is important but not relevant at the moment and disruptive to the flow and direction you're taking. Rather than just saying: "I'm glad you brought that up; we'll get to it later," you might label a flipchart sheet Parking Lot and capture their idea in a few words, along with their name or initials. Then, when the timing is more appropriate, you can address the issue. The "parking lot" serves as your reminder and tickler file. Cross off items as you take them up.

33. Avoid Judge or Referee Roles

When differences of opinions occur or when someone displays faulty logic (e.g., misconceptions, fallacies, or shaky conclusions), you may be tempted to correct them yourself. Instead, ask questions that lead the individual or the group to modify their stand: "How do the rest of you feel about Anne's point?" Or perhaps by something like this: "Okay, Tom. Let's suppose we follow your suggestion on the new incentive plan. How do you think the people in staff support positions are going to react when they find out about it?" Once you become the referee or the person with the answers, you've removed the responsibility from the group and taken it on yourself. You've disempowered them.

34. Use Your Participants as Resources

The better you can get to know the experience and background of your participants, the more you can tap that experience and direct questions and requests to them: "Tom, maybe you can answer Marianne's question; I believe you had some experience last year with that kind of situation in your area." Or perhaps: "Can any of you think of an example where Bill's idea has been tried before?"

35. Visualize to Make Points

A picture is worth thousands of words. Use the flipchart to illustrate a point. Simple models, diagrams, and illustrations help in ensuring that all your participants have the same picture in their heads. Encourage your participants to think of the flipchart as a large notepad that anyone can use to make a point. When pages will be valuable as later reference points, mount them on the walls and refer to them as appropriate. Summarize discussion with diagrams. Example: "We seem to be in agreement that three factors influence our effectiveness as a team: having the right people, doing the right work, and getting the right organizational support. Maybe I could illustrate this with a simple diagram." (Drawing on flipchart.) "Where

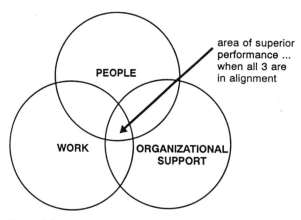

Figure 4.2

the three circles overlap and converge is where we are most effective. Now, how do you think we're doing as a team and an organization on getting the best alignment of these three circles?" (See Figure 4.2)

36. Use Humor

A relaxed, informal atmosphere is more conducive to effective discussion and participation than a formal or tense climate. However, you may have to facilitate a session in which issues are sensitive and people are tense. A light touch and spontaneous humor will go far in relaxing the group. The key word here is *spontaneous*—telling your three favorite jokes is probably not appropriate. If you know you're entering a hostile situation, you might start with levity: "What do you think is going to happen today? I've got the medics alerted and we have an ambulance standing by." Or if people were told to come and had no say in the matter, start with: "You know, people come to these sessions for one of three reasons. They were taken hostage, they want to escape a heavy workload, or they really want to be here and had nothing better to do. Let me see hands. How many of you were taken hostage—you were told to be here?"

Self-Quiz on Discussion Leadership Skills

1. Recall the discussions that have occurred at past meetings you've attended at work. What percentage of these discussions would you guess were successful? _____ . What criteria are you applying to measure their success?

2. Describe the two roles (extremes) that you might fill as discussion leader, and give an example of the types of meeting that might call for each role.

3. What are the the major factors that should influence your discussion leadership style?

4. How many of the 36 guidelines described in this chapter are relevant to the types of discussions you are responsible for conducting? _____ . In the space below, list the numbers of the guidelines that do not apply.

5. Which guidelines have you not applied much in the past but have targeted for use in leading future discussions?

6. How many of the 36 guidelines describe actions that any participant in a discussion might apply?

7. What actions can you take to increase the use of these techniques (by yourself and by participants) when you hold meetings and have discussions?

8. Refer to the model in Figure 4.1. For each of the three seating arrangements shown in Figure 4.3, indicate what style of leadership is appropriate in each arrangement.

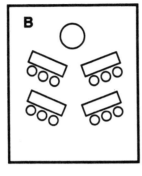
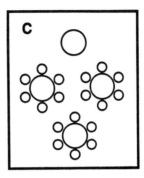

A

Style: _____

B

Style: _____

C

Style: _____

Figure 4.3

5 Using Questions Effectively

To be able to ask a question clearly is two-thirds of the way to getting it answered.

—*John Ruskin*

The decisions and actions you take depend on the quality of the information you obtain as input. Questions are the tools you use to obtain information and to involve others in the processes that strengthen teamwork: problem solving, decision making, benchmarking, setting goals and expectations, and evaluating performance.

In school, we received little if any instruction on how to use questions effectively. Courses on interviewing and survey research techniques usually deal with the skill of drafting questions, but most people have never learned how to use probes, confirm understanding, or phrase questions. As a result, we pose structured (directive) questions when unstructured (open-ended) ones would be more appropriate, and vice versa.

In this chapter, we'll put the magnifying glass on the question as a vital tool of facilitators. Specifically, upon completing chapter five you will be able to:

- Describe the advantages and drawbacks of using directive questions.
- Construct questions to deal with four types of problems at meetings.
- Convert inappropriate directive questions to appropriate nondirective ones.
- Use questions to restate or clarify contributions by participants.
- List at least a half dozen uses for questions (i.e., the purposes served).
- Prescreen the wording of questions to remove unintended bias.
- Classify the purpose of questions (in a script) as empathic, critical, searching, and advising.

- Evaluate questions (in a script) with regard to their effectiveness in achieving their objectives.

Questions are the most useful tool to get participants to contribute. You can direct a question to an individual: "Cathy, you've handled this kind of situation before. What benefits do you see in doing it the way George suggests?" Or you can use general questions that involve all participants: "What benefits can we list? And George, can I ask you to do our recording and write the benefits on the flipchart."

Lectures and briefings are never as satisfying as interactive sessions in which everyone gets into the act. Questions enable you to:

- Stimulate discussion with provocative questions that are used to initiate thought and maintain a lively interaction.
- Keep the discussion meaningful (i.e., relevant to the majority of participants and specific to the objectives and agenda).
- Get broader involvement and elicit the thinking of as many participants as possible.
- Provide facts, policy, and subject matter expertise as needed (from yourself or others in the group).

In virtually every meeting, there are a few outspoken participants who answer all the questions and carry on the discussion among themselves. It is not their intention to exclude others. Rather, it is human nature that some participants will be active and others passive—the 20–80 rule we spoke of earlier in guidelines 13.

Your role is not easy. On the one hand, you should not allow a few persons to answer all the questions. Yet you don't want to ignore them or to say anything to discourage them: "Let's not hear from the same people all the time. How about some others?"

Similarly, you do not want to embarrass those who are not participating. It is generally not advisable to say: "Paul, we haven't heard from you today. What do you think about this?" A better approach is to say: "Paul, I believe you've had some experience in handling this kind of problem in your department. What's your advice?"

One of the most frequent reasons for using questions is to direct the group's attention to issues that they are not taking into account: "I wonder if there's any relevance to the fact that. . . ." As mentioned previously, however, you don't want to do the thinking for your participants. Rather, you want to nudge them with a gentle clue to discover for themselves the issue they have overlooked.

The table in Figure 5.1 lists some of the situations that require direction on your part and provides sample questions that can help steer discussion and keep the session productive.

Situation	Sample Question
Participants are going down a side street on an unimportant issue.	How much importance do you think we should attach to this issue?
All available information has not been given; you want to remind them without leading.	I wonder if we've gotten all the information needed for us to reach a decision?
The discussion is wandering from the point; you want to bring it back.	What point are we now considering?
A summary of group consensus is needed before moving on.	I wonder if someone could summarize, maybe at the flipchart, the points on which we agree and disagree?
You feel that the group is not ready to take action.	When do you think we will be ready to reach a decision and take action?
Two opposing factions are having trouble reaching agreement.	Where on the continuum between these two points of view does the best course of action lie?"
The group is prejudiced or acting in self-interest.	I wonder if our own interest in the outcome might be causing us to overlook the interest of other groups?

Figure 5.1

Restating and Clarifying

Group participants typically vary in verbal ability. Some have no difficulty in putting their thoughts into words and getting ideas across to the group. With those who might be less articulate, lack organization, or feel overshadowed by others present, it's your job to translate. The following list suggests tactful ways of doing this that won't embarrass the participant:

- Restatement by you: If I understand you correctly, Priscilla, you're saying that . . ..
- Restatement by participant: Let's make sure everyone understands the point you're making, Janet. Would you summarize it for us?
- Restatement by another participant: I'm not sure I understand the point that George is making. Would one of you clarify it for me?
- Direct questioning: What you're saying, Mrs. Thomkins, raises a question or two in my mind. For example, do you . . ..
- Reaction of participants: How do the rest of you feel about Phil's comments? (The feedback of the participants will tell Phil what they did and didn't understand about his contribution.)

The persons who are not getting a point across are often not aware of their trouble. You are in a better position to recognize that others in the group do not understand. This is why it's important for you to seek clarification in a way that doesn't embarrass.

Other participants ramble on and on with needless restatement and elaboration and run the point into the ground. You must interrupt. Otherwise these persons might keep the floor, monopolize the meeting, and waste precious time. You can turn them off tactfully with something like this: "Good point, Harry! Let's see how the rest of the group feels about it, or whether there are some other points that we should hear before reaching a decision." Here's another way of dealing with the rambler: "Let me interrupt, Grace, to see if I've understood your point. You feel that . . . ." Your brief summary of Grace's comments should bring closure to her contribution.

One of the biggest challenges of being an effective facilitator and discussion leader is to ensure that the participants do not get bogged down in trivial details on the one hand or become superficial on the other hand. Members are sometimes willing to settle for partial solutions, insights, or principles because they fail to take all the issues or information into account . . . especially if they are anxious to bring the meeting to a close and get out of there.

Because you have had more time and experience than your participants in exploring the issues present, you may have a natural temptation to give away the correct solutions or rush the group to reach the outcome you are looking for. But this does not help to develop your participants' ability as critical thinkers, problem solvers, and decision makers. Nor does it get their commitment through involvement. You can only move as fast as their ability and willingness will allow.

Avoiding Built-In Bias

Any question you ask is in danger of having a built-in bias that will give your participants some clue as to the type of response you're looking for. The question, "George, do you think we should have a better performance appraisal system than the old one now in use?" has a high degree of bias—it lets George know that you're expecting a yes from him. In fact, any question that has only two answers (e.g., yes-no, true-false, does-doesn't, or more-less) is biased by its very nature, in that there are often other alternatives that are not allowed for in the wording of the question—the truth often lies in the grey area between white and black.

This is not to say that yes-no questions are not useful during a meeting. Indeed, their major use comes from their ability to polarize—that is, to split the group into two sides on an issue. As participants discuss these two sides, they usually realize that the truth lies somewhere between. This type of behavior occurs in any activity in which there is give and take and where a win-win outcome is only possible through compromise (e.g., price negotiations, grievance procedures and arbitration, and performance appraisal).

Almost any question posed to the group could have been phrased in different ways, depending on how much structure and direction you wish to give your listeners. Figure 5.2 compares directive and nondirective wordings of the same questions.

Directive	Nondirective
Bob, do you really expect the group to go along with your point?	What do the rest of you think about the point Bob just made?
Agnes, don't you think that's off the topic?	Agnes, can you help us relate your comment to the topic we're discussing?
You don't have any facts to support that position, do you? (Strong no implied as answer.)	Let's listen now to some of the facts that support that position.
I guess we're all in agreement to recommend this program to management.	How do you feel about recommending this program to management?
Should all employees belong to self-directed work teams in the long run?	How does one decide which employees or work units should belong to self-directed work teams?
Do you think the employees will accept the new faces this merger will bring? (Strong no implied as answer.)	How do you think the employees will react to the new faces?

Figure 5.2

To summarize, your role as discussion leader is to serve as a catalyst, stimulating and guiding discussion, suggesting its direction rather than pushing or pulling, talking with participants rather than at them, and serving as a resource, consultant, or catalyst but never dominating or lecturing.

The word *facilitator* is replacing the word *leader* when applied to the person conducting a meeting or training session. Your role is to make it easy for the group you are facilitating to learn, solve problems, or reach decisions. You can't do it for them.

Asking Effective Questions

Questions can be used to arouse interest, to confirm understanding, or to lead the group to discover a principle or work out a solution on their own.

Let's look at a brief dialogue between a facilitator and a group of participants who have just gone through the response style exercise you completed in chapter 2.

Dialogue		Purpose of Question
Facilitator:	Have you all added up the points and gotten your scores on the response style exercise? Does anyone need more time?	To keep the group together, to manage time effectively.
Participants:	(No verbal response, but participants look up. No one is doing calculations, so facilitator continues.)	
Facilitator:	Who wants to take a guess on how you came out as a group? What would you guess your highest and next highest styles might be?	To arouse interest in what is coming.
Participants:	(Several participants take guesses.)	
Facilitator:	Okay. I'd like you to raise your hand when I mention your highest score. How many had searching as their highest score? (Hands) How many had critical? (Hands) Empathic? (Hands) And advising? (Hands)	To assess group members' predominant styles.
Participant:	I had a tie between my two highest scores. How should I handle that?	
Facilitator:	How did you handle it?	To help participants answer their own questions (deductive strategy).
Participant:	I held up my hand twice.	
Facilitator:	Good thinking. Now, if I counted your hands correctly, it looks as if searching is the big one, and advising came in second. How many remember from your assignment last night the two types of interpersonal relationships that these four response styles illustrate? Let's see hands, please.	To find out whether the homework got done, so as to build on it or not (class management).
Participants:	(More than half raise their hands, so facilitator continues.)	
Facilitator:	I'd like you to turn to your neighbor and answer this question: Which two styles are parent-to-child by nature? And which two are adult-to-adult? Take half a minute to compare answers.	To confirm understanding—this is feedback to the facilitator and reinforcement to the participants.

Using Questions Effectively

Dialogue		Purpose of Question
Participants:	(Working in pairs, participants answer to their neighbors while facilitator circulates to listen in on a number of answers.)	
Facilitator:	Okay. May I have your attention again, please. Let's reconvene, please. Marge, what did you and Joe say were the two response styles that are adult-to-adult by nature?	To use participants as a resource (to elicit the learning points from the group).
Participant: (Marge)	We said that the Searching and the Empathic responses are adult responses.	
Facilitator:	Which means the Critical and Advising responses are parent-to-child by nature. Do you all agree with that? Did anyone come out differently?	To confirm understanding—this is feedback to the instructor and reinforcement to the learners.
Participant: (Harry)	Tom and I had trouble deciding whether the empathic response is adult or parent. Marge called it adult, but I see a lot of parents showering their kids with empathy and sometimes mothering them to death.	
Facilitator:	Let's address Harry's concern. What's the difference between empathy and sympathy? Can anyone help us here? Yes, Cindy.	To get participants to help one another (deductive strategy).
Participant: (Cindy)	Well, empathy is showing feeling for someone or being sensitive to how they feel. And sympathy is being sorry for them or showing pity for them.	
Facilitator:	Well put. Empathy says, I want to understand how you feel. Or, I think I see where you're coming from. Whereas sympathy says, You poor thing, I feel sorry for you. Now then, is sympathy a parent-to-child response or an adult-to-adult response? Anyone?	To draw a conclusion and reach closure (summary point).
Participants:	Parent-to-child.	(same as above)
Facilitator:	And is empathy a parent-to-child response or an adult-to-adult response?	
Participants:	Adult-to-adult.	
Facilitator:	Exactly. Sympathy is judgmental, and can interfere with your objectivity. Because empathy is nonjudgmental, it won't affect your objectivity. Now, Harry, you and Tom weren't sure whether empathy was a parent response or an adult one	To lead a participant to correct a misconception.

55

Dialogue		Purpose of Question
	because you've seen a lot of parents showering their kids with empathy and mothering them. Was that an example of empathy or sympathy?	
Participant: (Harry)	Okay. I see the problem. We were confusing the two. Sympathy is a parent-type response, but empathy is adult.	
Facilitator:	You got it! Now when I asked for a show of hands a few minutes ago, Searching came in first, and Searching is an adult response. But Advising, which came in as your second most common way of responding, is a parent-to-child response. Does that bother anyone? Isn't it desirable to avoid parent-type responses?	To see if participants understand the pitfalls of advising (needs analysis).
Participant:	They're not always bad, are they?	
Facilitator:	Good question. What do you think?	To let a participant make a point.
Participant:	Sometimes it's necessary to give criticism or advice, isn't it?	
Facilitator:	Sometimes, yes. But in most cases, no. And it's sometimes hard to resist giving advice because the people you work with often turn to you for it. What's wrong with giving advice? Take a piece of paper and write down one or two undesirable things that can happen when you give a person advice.	To get information about the group
Participants:	(While participants write, facilitator circulates to look over the responses. Facilitator then reconvenes the group.)	
Facilitator:	As I looked over your responses, I saw a lot of good thinking on the pitfalls or dangers of giving advice. In fact, let me record your responses at the flipchart. Who wants to start me off with something you wrote?	To use participants as a resource (to elicit the learning points from the group).
Participants:	Responses from different participants, including: • People depend on you instead of themselves. • If your advice doesn't work, you get blamed. • There's no commitment if there's no authorship. • People learn best by solving their own problems.	

The facilitator continued, drawing the conclusion that two response styles maintain adult interactions (Searching, or getting more information, and Empathic, or showing concern for the thoughts and feelings of others). These develop "I'm okay, You're okay" relationships. The other two response styles (Critical and Advising) perpetuate parent-to-child interactions and thus tend to develop "I'm okay, You're not okay" relationships.

The meeting could have been for supervisors, members of a self-directed work team, or any other group that is concerned with improved communication skills. For our purposes, the audience and the content are not important. Our focus is on process, and the fact that questions are often more effective than statements in influencing the thoughts and actions of others.

The Purpose of a Question

The purpose of a question is to get information. The purpose of a screwdriver is to turn a screw. But tools can be used for many purposes—there are probably at least a half dozen other uses to which you have put screwdrivers. Similarly, if the question is to be our most useful tool as facilitators, we should be adept at applying it in as many ways as it will effectively serve us. Here are some of the more common ways:

- **To test understanding.** Used when you need to assess the participants' levels of comprehension; for example: "What would happen if . . . ?"
- **To make a point.** Used to influence participants to think in a certain way; for example: "Do you think that the average employee is only interested in pay?"
- **To lead participants to discover.** Used when teaching deductively; for example: "What are some of the pitfalls of giving advice when someone asks for it?"
- **To stimulate creative thinking.** Used when brainstorming; for example: "How can we get greater employee involvement in our work group meetings?"
- **To assess needs of the group.** Used when deciding how much experience the participants have; for example: "How many of you have ever had to . . . ?"
- **To arouse interest in the topic.** Used to elicit a guess; for example: "What percentage of your time is spent listening in a typical day at work?"
- **To encourage introspection.** Used to help participants analyze their behavior; for example: "What qualities do you possess that have helped you as a project manager?"
- **To ventilate.** Used to address and dispel negative attitudes; for example:

"What kinds of flack might we expect from our employees when we announce . . . ?"
- **To poll the group.** Used to reach consensus, get feedback, or test the water; for example: "How many of you feel that we should . . . ?"
- **To rephrase a participant's question.** Used when the group doesn't understand a participant's question; for example: "Are you asking whether we should . . . ?"
- **To steer the group.** Used when participants are going astray or not managing time effectively; for example: "How much more time do you want to spend on this issue?"
- **To get participant to answer his or her own question.** Used when participant was really making a point by asking a question; for example: "Good question. What do **you** think?"
- **To summarize and get closure.** Used to wrap up a meeting; for example: "Now let's summarize. What are the five ways of dealing with a problem?"

The following is a script of a meeting that Rudy, a team facilitator, had with Ted, one of the people he is counseling. Use the Notes column to enter your comments on what you do and don't like about the way Rudy handled the session. Then answer the questions that follow the script.

Self-Quiz on Using Questions Effectively

Directions: In the Notes column to the right of the script, indicate with a few words what you do and don't like about the way Rudy dealt with Ted. In other words, each time Rudy speaks (the odd-numbered lines), give your evaluation of the appropriateness of Rudy's comment and your suggested wording (i.e, what you would like Rudy to have said).

Dialogue		Notes
1. Rudy:	I just had a call from Mr. Sewell. He said that one of his people called you about expediting an order and you refused. What's the story?	
2. Ted:	Mario called me. When I tried to tell him what work I had ahead of the order, he told me that was my problem and if I didn't want Mr. Sewell on my tail, I'd better push the order through.	
3. Rudy:	What did you tell him?	
4. Ted:	I told him to shove it. He'll get it when he gets it.	

5. Rudy: You told him to shove it?

6. Ted: Yeah. I've got a pile this high (he demonstrates) on my desk, and I can't stop my other work just for them.

7. Rudy: Do you think that's the way we should respond to other employees who come to us for help?

8. Ted: No, and I don't need a lecture. I know I've been a bad boy. But if you had to put up with Mario's pushy manner, you'd lose your cool, too.

9. Rudy: But that's no reason to add fuel to his fire. What you should have done is find out when he has to have it by—at the latest. Then see if you can get it to him with your normal flow of taking the orders in sequence.

10. Ted: He said he needed it immediately—that's what they all say. What we need is a system for stamping the time we receive each order so that we . . .

11. Rudy: (interrupting) What we need is a little courtesy. Now I've got to call Mr. Sewell back and apologize, or maybe you should, since you caused the mess. No, I'll do it, since it was me he called. What do you want me to tell him?

12. Ted: Tell him I'm swamped with orders, but that I'll interrupt everything to dig out his lousy order and send it over.

13. Rudy: Good. And next time Mario calls, don't be so childish. Try to count slowly to 10 before you get us both in deep water. Okay?

14. Ted: Okay.

Rudy's Questioning Skills

1. What do you think of the way Rudy began his counseling session with Ted (line 1)? Would you have started the talk differently?

2. During the first half of his talk with Ted, Rudy asked questions (lines 1, 3, 5, 7). Was this appropriate?

3. On the basis of your reading of the script, what do you think Rudy's objectives are in having a counseling session with Ted? Are they appropriate?

4. How well do you think Rudy has achieved his objectives (i.e., on the basis of Ted's responses)?

5. Suppose that you have been asked to design a form to help managers, supervisors, counselors, and personnel specialists prepare for a counseling session—a tool to improve their ability to deal with a problem employee (i.e., one whose behavior is out of line and deviating from the established norms). What questions or issues would you list and in what sequence?

6. The comments that Rudy made during his counseling session might be classified as any one of the following:
    - Critical (C)—finding fault, blaming.
    - Advising (A)—telling someone what to do.
    - Searching (S)—asking for more information.
    - Empathic (E)—showing understanding.

   Reread each of Rudy's comments and label each with one or more of the four letters noted above to indicate Rudy's intent on each comment.

   1. _____
   3. _____
   5. _____
   7. _____
   9. _____

11. _____

13. _____

7. Our interactions with other humans are conducted on either a parent-to-child basis or an adult-to-adult basis. The critical response (C) is the hallmark of a judgmental parent, while the advising response (A) is typical of a nurturing parent. Each one treats the other person like a child. The searching and empathic responses, (S) and (E), are adult responses that treat the other person as a fellow adult.

   Looking again at Rudy's responses that you labeled above, to what degree was the counseling session conducted on an adult-to-adult basis?

8. When should a counseling session be conducted on a parent-to-child basis? When should it be adult-to-adult?

Rudy's Questioning Skills: Answers to Previous Questions

Now it's time to compare your answers to the eight questions relating to Rudy's counseling skills with ours.

1. Rudy began with a quick, objective, neutral (unbiased) statement of the situation as described by Mario's boss, Mr. Sewell. No problem here. It would be wrong for Rudy to start with small talk or anything that would delay getting to the point. If you feel that Rudy's "and you refused" is a critical comment, this phrase could be dropped. Either way, Rudy's initial comment should get Ted doing the talking. His first step is to find out what happened so that he can assess the situation.
2. Yes. Questions are Rudy's most useful tool for getting the information needed to assess the situation. Rudy is in the fact-finding phase of their talk. However, although his first two questions (Lines 1 and 3) are neutral and adult-to-adult, he then asks questions that are biased and parent-to-child (Lines 5 and 7). These move the session from fact-finding to fault-finding, putting Ted on the defensive.

3. Although Rudy would probably tell us that his objective was to correct the situation, the script suggests that Rudy also wanted to reprimand Ted. This may get in the way of correcting the situation and reducing the likelihood of a similar recurrence down the road. And these are the objectives that we feel are appropriate.
4. Ted's responses are those of a naughty child, alternately accepting and rejecting blame. "I know I've been a bad boy" and "If you had to put up with..." and "What we need is a system for...." Yes, Ted has agreed to process Mario's order, but mainly to get Rudy off his back. And relations between Mario and Ted will probably be worse than ever.
5. There is no single set of questions that would be the correct way to counsel a problem employee. The questions noted below are but one way of handling the assignment. So don't expect your list to agree with ours.

    What you want to check for in evaluating your questions is the degree to which they meet the following criteria:

    - they maintain an adult-to-adult interaction; and
    - they are deductive, leading the employee to realize the problem and take responsibility for correcting it.

    Example:

    (a) I need your help. We've got a problem that's being caused by your... (description of deviant behavior). Were you aware that this is causing a problem?
    (b) What are some of the undesirable consequences that your actions might be causing?
    (c) Are there any unusual circumstances or factors that led you to act this way? Is there anything I should know?
    (d) Now that we've identified the problem, the consequences of it, and the contributing causes, what action do you see as appropriate to correct the situation?
    (e) How will you go about this? When? How will we know that the problem has been corrected?

6. Here's how we have rated Rudy's intent on each comment:
    Comment No.
    1. S, although you may have seen "and you refused" as C.
    3. S.
    5. C or S, depending on tone of voice and facial expression.
    7. C.
    9. C and A.
    11. C, ending with S.
    13. C.

7. Only at the start (fact-finding stage) was the counseling session conducted on an adult-to-adult basis. However, after the first 4 to 6 lines, the dialogue lapsed into scolding and blaming, with Rudy blaming Ted and Ted blaming everything else: the workload, Mario's pushy manner, the lack of a system for stamping the time as orders are received.
8. Unlike sessions in which the purpose is to discipline or reprimand, a counseling session should be conducted on an adult-to-adult basis. This is not easy, because the person being counseled may find it difficult to accept the fact that there is a problem or that his or her behavior has not been appropriate. (Mark Twain once noted that there is no such thing as constructive criticism; the phrase is an oxymoron.)

    We believe that all counseling should be conducted on an adult-to-adult basis to be effective. Even if the person being counseled responds as a parent or child, the counselor should remain in the adult state and not let the interaction lapse into an emotional bout whose outcome is win-lose at best and lose-lose at worst.

How did your answers compare with ours? What have you learned about the use of questions? What insights have you gained about your own style and skill in counseling people? What actions, if any, do you plan to take to improve your coaching and counseling skills?

Rudy's Questioning Skills: Evaluation and Feedback

Here is a script of the way Rudy's meeting with Ted should have been handled. As you read the script of their meeting, refer to our notes in the margin to the right of the script. Notice the techniques that Rudy is now applying and how effective they are in getting Ted's cooperation and willingness to correct the situation.

Notes

1 Rudy:	I just had a call from Mr. Sewell. He said that one of his people called you about expediting an order and you refused. What's the story?	
2 Ted:	Mario called me. When I tried to tell him what work I had ahead of the order, and that it meant a lot of extra work for me to dig it out, he told me that that was my problem and if I didn't want Mr. Sewell on my tail, I'd better push the order through.	*Lines 1 and 3 are fact-finding in nature. Rudy is simply asking Ted what happened.*
3 Rudy:	What did you tell him?	

4 Ted: I told him to shove it. He'll get it when he gets it.

5 Rudy: Now, you say it would mean a lot of extra work for you to dig out the order. I've always felt that you were very effective at finding orders that are buried in the process file.

Rather than criticizing Ted for his response to Mario, Rudy remains adult and continues to deal with facts rather than with emotions. Lines 5 and 7 combine the empathic and the searching responses.

6 Ted: Well, it's no big deal to find his order. I just don't like people telling me how to do my job.

7 Rudy: I can't blame you for that—no one likes that. What is the status of your current work load?

8 Ted: I've got a pile this high (he demonstrates) on my desk, and I can't stop my other work just for them.

9 Rudy: Okay. We've found the problem. Mario's request interrupts your regular work, and his manner of asking leaves something to be desired. You already have a heavy backlog of work. As a result, you told him off, which has now led to getting Mr. Sewell and me into the act. Is that a fair description of the situation?

Line 9 lets Ted know that this talk has problem solving and not reprimand as its objective. Although Rudy's "you told him off" acknowledges Ted's inappropriate behavior, there is no blame or scolding in his message. He returns in lines 11 and 13 to a searching or information getting response.

10 Ted: Yeah. That's about the size of it.

11 Rudy: What are our options at this point?

12 Ted: Well, I guess I better go back and find the order and send them the stuff. Otherwise I'll have Mr. Sewell and you on my tail.

13 Rudy: When does he need the stuff?

14 Ted: He said immediately—they all say that. What we need is a system for stamping the time we receive each order, so we can prioritize special requests based on what the backlog is and not promise what we can't deliver. Sometimes I ask people what the latest time is that they must have it by. I guess I should have asked him this.

15 Rudy: That's a good question to ask.

Rudy's treatment of Ted as an adult rather than a child brings out the information needed to solve the problem. In line 15, Rudy acknowledges this.

16 Ted: And maybe I'd have had enough time to process his order in the normal flow of taking the orders in sequence.

17 Rudy: Good thinking. And I like your idea of stamping the time and date of each order received. I wasn't aware that we weren't doing that already.

In lines 17 and 19, Rudy treats Ted on an adult-to-adult basis, thereby eliciting responsible adult behavior on Ted's part. This is important to the solution of the problem that Rudy set out to identify and solve.

18 Ted: It's not my idea. We used to do it when Joe was here. But then, well, I don't know why we dropped it.

19 Rudy: You know, Ted, with your experience around here, I think you're just the one to get it going again. Do you think you could find that old sheet that outlined the procedures or make up another one if you can't find it? I know you're buried in orders right now, so there's no hurry; it could be done next week if this week is bad.

20 Ted: Yeah. I can do that. And I've got some ideas on how to improve the old system.

21 Rudy: Great. Let me see it when you've got it together—say by Thursday of next week. Okay?

In Lines 21 and 23, Rudy now has an action plan. He knows what each party must do to correct the problem. Notice that in both lines, Rudy is using the searching response (asking questions) to make sure that Ted is committed and will deliver on his part of the agreement.

From Managing to Empowering

Notes

22 Ted: Okay. And I may have it ready sooner.

23 Rudy: All the better. Well, I promised Mr. Sewell I'd call him back, so I'll tell him you're pulling his order together now and that Mario will have it within the next two hours. That will please him. Anything else I should tell him?

24 Ted: (pause) Yeah, tell him I'm sorry I blew my cool.

6 Roles And Responsibilities

A leader must face danger, take risk and blame, and help followers to understand and deal with tempests in the storm. Yet great leaders never set themselves above their followers except in one regard: acceptance of their roles and responsibilities as pilot of the ship, helping the passengers to ride out the storm and reach shore safely.

All the books we've ever read on how to run a meeting or lead a group discussion begin with the same advice: Set your objectives, identify the desired outcomes, and agree on the activities and agenda needed to accomplish your objectives. This is one of the roles and responsibilities of an effective facilitator, but only one.

Rarely does a meeting take place in which the objectives and agenda remain unchanged. Participants have their own needs and concerns—that is, their own objectives and agendas. These range from minor crosscurrents in the mainstream of a discussion to major tempests and storms that can prevent the group from reaching the desired outcomes.

In this chapter, we'll examine 12 roles and responsibilities that facilitators should be prepared to fill. As you go through the suggestions that accompany each, make notes in the margin beside those that you plan to add to your repertoire of discussion leadership skills. In addition, if you plan to give training to group participants on how to have more productive sessions, you might want to indicate which suggestions should be shared with the group and practiced at subsequent meetings.

More specifically, upon completing chapter 6 you will be able to:

- Set goals and objectives for meetings, preferably in advance and in writing.

- Maintain focus and flow by using integrating and unifying statements.
- Rephrase and clarify contributions to improve understanding and retention.
- Deflect and return questions that participants should be able to handle.
- Make use of the six techniques for relieving group tension.
- Set limits on time allotment, participation, and roles (i.e., for the task force and the individual).
- Draw on at least five ways to get all members participating.
- Initiate action to remove roadblocks or diversions to your main objectives.
- Serve as a resource by asking questions rather than giving advice.
- Establish the structure, ground rules, and limits to authority.
- Give closure by summarizing accomplishments and future action: who will do what.

During the course of a meeting, the discussion and group interaction pass through different stages that demand a variety of leadership skills. In a mature group—that is, one that recognizes that a successful outcome depends on everyone present—these demands may be handled by members of the group.

However, in a newly formed group or one in which the purpose and outcome depend on the expertise or rank of the person in charge, the discussion leader must steer the group and handle the challenges that arise. Here are a dozen of the more common roles and responsibilities that group leaders should be prepared to handle:

- Goal setting and resetting
- Integrating and focusing
- Rephrasing and clarifying
- Deflecting and returning
- Relieving tension
- Setting limits
- Increasing participation
- Initiating action
- Serving as a resource
- Structuring
- Handling problem participants
- Summarizing and follow-up

Goal Setting and Resetting

Whenever possible, the goals (i.e., the purpose, objective, or desired outcomes) of a meeting should be made known to participants before they arrive. This enables them to arrive prepared by bringing material with them or reading a background memo or report. The leader should also start the meeting by summarizing the goals to be met. Sometimes it's appropriate to write these on a flipchart or distribute a handout that states the purpose and desired outcome of the meeting.

One advantage of putting the goals in writing is that you can refer to them if the discussion begins to wander and participants bring up issues that are not relevant: "I'm having trouble relating our comments of the last few minutes to the goals we agreed to at the start. Can someone help me to see the connection?"

Another way of returning a discussion that has gone afield is to summarize or ask someone else to do so: "Perhaps it would be useful at this point to take inventory of what we've accomplished and what remains to be done if we're to meet the goals we set at the start. Who can summarize for us?"

Integrating and Focusing

This function is your way of helping the discussion achieve coherence, unity, and flow. Often participants will contribute comments that may seem unrelated or rambling. Your job is to see the intent behind such remarks and to integrate them with a unifying statement. Here's an example:

Bobbie: When my team has its weekly meeting, most of the suggestions we've submitted for improvement haven't been acted upon by the management committee. Why clog the pipeline with more suggestions?

Jean: My people are beginning to ask me if they can be excused from attending our weekly meetings due to other deadlines and their heavy workload.

Paul: I read the other day that a lot of companies are having trouble making work teams work once the original excitement dies down and the honeymoon is over. Members feel that they are spinning their wheels and rehashing old stuff at their meetings.

Leader: It sounds like we're saying that the weekly meetings are not as productive as they should be. Employees are frustrated by the lack of progress from week to week.

Going further, if you sense the purpose behind their comments, your integrating summary might attempt to bring the intent into the open. In this example, the leader might continue with:

Leader: I wonder if the problem is that once a week is too frequent a schedule for our team meetings, and that every other week or even once a month might be more productive. What do you think?

Rephrasing and Clarifying

As a discussion leader, you help clarify the content of group contributions by noting certain statements so the speaker and the group can examine them in depth. Here are some of the more common reasons you would do this:

- You'd like the contributor and other participants to realize that a statement is a gross overgeneralization.
- The contribution is based on faulty reasoning (e.g., false premises, shaky conclusions, fallacies, or non sequiturs).
- The statement contradicts earlier thoughts or actions the group agreed to and you want to see if they realize the inconsistency.
- You doubt that the contributor meant to say what the group just heard, so you rephrase to give the contributor a chance to retract or modify.
- A participant has just made a key point that you'd like to emphasize and to anchor in the group's memory, so you restate or rephrase the point.

As discussion leaders, we typically have certain objectives to be met and certain points we hope the participants will bring up during the discussion. We thus face the risk of taking a participant's contribution that is similar to a point we're looking for and rephrasing it in a way that makes our point. But it may not have been the speaker's point at all. Rephrasing is appropriate, preceded by: Bill, you seem to feel that . . . , Jan, are you saying that . . . , or Ted, let me see if I understand. You think that . . . . However, be careful not to modify the content or intent of the contribution. Its ownership should not change hands from the contributor to you.

Deflecting and Returning

Sometimes participants direct questions to the leader that should be returned to the group, deflected to an expert, or rescheduled to give the leader time to prepare an answer. Here are some examples. (Assume in each situation that the question was relevant to the purpose of the meeting.)

These examples illustrate some of the ways you have of reminding the group that everyone is responsible for the success of your meeting. Participants have had years of conditioning that place the burden on the person up front (e.g., school, church, town council, business meetings, or entertainment). It's easy for them to lapse into the role of spectator and observe you in action. Deflection and returning are techniques that accept their questions and concerns as relevant, but then shift the responsibility back

Questions to be Deflected or Returned	Suggestions for Handling such Questions
Sam: With that crazy new policy on overtime, there's no way we can meet our production quotas. Do they honestly expect us to?	Probably a rhetorical question intended to blow off steam or score points with other participants. Show empathy, perhaps laugh, but don't take sides: Sam, that's the question we'd all like an answer to.
Marge: What do you think of the design of the 1997 model that they just unveiled? Do you think it will recapture our share of market?	The person asking has some strong opinions, or the question wouldn't have been posed. Give them the floor: Marge, you've evidently seen the design. What do you think of it?
Joe: You want us to deal with others on an adult-to-adult basis. How can you do that when your boss treats you on a parent-to-child basis?	A great opportunity to get the group involved: I'm sure Joe isn't the only one to have ever faced this situation. Is it possible? Or is it always a like-father, like-son situation?
Ann: With the ceiling on spending, I can't replace any of my obsolete equipment. Any idea when it will be lifted?	Ann, my understanding is that the ceiling applies to nonessential spending. George, you just got a requisition for new equipment approved, didn't you?
Bob: If we volunteer for a reduced-hour workweek, will that make it less likely or more likely that our names will be on the next list of layoffs?	A serious question and you don't know the answer: Bob, let me check with HR and see if I can have an answer for you next time we meet. You might try to have someone from HR take 10 minutes of your next meeting.
Terry: Is it better for us to ... A ... or to ... B? Which should we do?	Terry, you'll be ready to answer that question yourself after our session dealing with A and B. So let's hold the question 'til then.
Jan: What's the best way to apply for a job on the open posting on the bulletin board without bending your boss out of shape or messing up your future with him if you don't get the job?	Wow! That's a million dollar question. Who's got some ideas? Has anyone done this and kept peace with your boss? Let's see what suggestions we can come up with.
Harry: But we don't have access to that information at our terminals. You need a special code to get that out of classified, don't you?	Let's ask Marianne, our computer guru. Can you answer Harry's question?

to the individual or the group, thus maintaining your role as catalyst and avoiding the role of star performer.

Relieving Tension

Discussions can become heated. Issues get steamy and emotional, and personalities come under fire. Anger, blame, denial, frustration, and a host of other unhealthy reactions replace order, reason, progress, and control.

What can you do to relieve tension when you see it beginning to mount? Here are a few suggestions:

- Set ground rules at the start about what kinds of issues and behavior are appropriate and inappropriate. This enables you to interrupt when the discussion begins to enter forbidden territory.
- Tell the group up front that we want the room temperature to be comfortable . . . not too hot and not too cold. The moment a participant begins to get emotional, anyone can say, "I think it's getting hot in here . . . is anyone else warm?" Similarly, if a participant makes an off-color contribution or a sexist remark, anyone can say "I think it's getting cold in here . . . does anyone feel the chill?" (Of course, the best way to relieve tension caused by an inappropriate remark might be to ignore it. In some groups, this is appropriate, but in a team that is committed to growth and self-improvement, correction is called for.)
- Humor is the best antidote for tension because it diverts attention and provides comedy relief. The trick, of course, is to keep it relevant and short; for example: At a workshop, an Englishman from the home office in the U.K. was challenged by one of the American participants: "Could you repeat that? I didn't understand half of what you said." "Which half?" the Englishman replied. "Were you speaking English?" said the American, whose company was recently taken over by the British parent company. "Well, I certainly wasn't speaking American," came the testy retort. The group was tense. Time for humor from the discussion leader: "What we have here is a beautiful example of Winston Churchill's sage observation that 'England and the United States are two countries separated by the barrier of a common language!' I think the point we were discussing had to do with . . .".
- Someone is embarrassed at having misspelled a word on the flipchart or a handout. Rescue them with this quote: Mark Twain once observed that it is the mark of a very narrow person to be able to think of only one way to spell a given word.
- Acknowledge that disagreement is natural and often healthy because it stimulates thinking. Suggest that we can agree to disagree, and move on. If the group is well educated, quote Voltaire, who once said to someone, "I disagree completely with everything you have just said, but I will defend with my dying breath your right to say it." Or, if you'd like a more homespun example, Ben Franklin and a friend had a long-standing difference of opinion. Each would look for evidence to support his stand, then mail it to the other. Ben was the more tenacious and eloquent, leading to the last letter he ever received on the matter: "Ben, I surrender. You have won your case—and lost a friend."
- Interrupt long enough to point out that the direction we're moving is not relevant to our objectives and the issue isn't going to be resolved by further discussion, so let's return to the topic.

Setting Limits

Whether you are conducting a training session, leading a self-directed team, or running a meeting (planning and scheduling, problem solving, decision making, etc.), your role as leader is to set limits. We've already examined one example of setting limits: goal setting and resetting. The group's discussion, decisions, and actions should be supportive of (and limited by) the goals that were established at the start.

Time limits should also be made known at the start (i.e., in the schedule or agenda). As leaders, we must respect the fact that our participants have other things to do in addition to attending the sessions we facilitate. Letting people know when a meeting will end and what time frame has been allocated for each activity or topic enables participants to manage their time and not feel like unwilling hostages who have no control of time.

Because the success of a meeting or a discussion depends on having the right faces in the right places, it's desirable to set limits on who should and shouldn't attend. On certain kinds of meetings, different participants may have certain responsibilities and assignments. They should know in advance what expectations you and the group have of them.

The following form serves as a meeting planning sheet and announcement form. Notice the limits that have been set: ending time, responsibilities, schedule of activities, objectives, and participants. A blank copy of this form also appears in the Appendix, along with our permission to reproduce it if you feel it applies to some of the types of meetings you facilitate.

There's another meaning to setting limits. Some leaders find it useful to get the group's agreement on some basic ground rules governing their behavior in meetings. These guidelines relate mainly to procedural issues (e.g., don't interrupt, do express your ideas and opinions, or don't ramble or digress or monopolize). But they may also relate to content issues (e.g., don't discuss contractual issues, irrelevant items not on the agenda, personal issues, or time-consuming illustrations). You may find it helpful to distribute a sheet containing guidelines and limits relating to the group's behavior in meetings; an example is included in the Appendix.

Increasing Participation

As we've mentioned, the members of a group vary in their willingness and ability to participate. Typically a few persons are the outspoken ones and the others are content to observe. Yet the success of a meeting is closely related to the level of participation: the more involved your group mem-

MEETING ANNOUNCEMENT/AGENDA

Subject: Proposal from Component A
Today's Date: Oct. 28
Meeting Date/Time: Nov 1 / 8:30 AM
Duration: approximately 2 hours
Place: Room 1152
Confirm by Calling: Susan on 55432

Meeting Leaders: Frank

Participants:
Tom
Sharon
Chris
Mike
Pat

Desired Outcomes:

- To identify the pros and cons of absorbing workload from Component A
- To identify at least two possible alternatives to absorbing the workload directly into our operation
- To develop a list of additional information required before we can respond to Component A's proposal

Background Materials:
Please read proposal from Component A (attached)

Please Bring:
- Summary of workload/employee
- Current overtime schedule
- List of pending projects
- Projected personnel changes

Order of Agenda Items	Persons Responsible	Process	Time Allocated
• Factors surrounding Component A's proposal	Frank	Report	10 min.
• Pros and cons of the proposal	Tom	Brainstorm	30 min.
• Alternative actions (at least two)	Chris	Discussion and consensus decision	30 min.
• Additional information/back up required	Mike	Rank order from list of pros and cons	40 min.

bers become, the more likely you are to achieve your objectives and to adjourn with a high level of satisfaction among participants.

Your role is to increase participation without causing embarrassment or discomfort. Here are some of the ways you can accomplish this:

- Before the meeting, make assignments that spread the leadership role among the participants so that different persons are responsible for providing information (content and input) or leading the discussion (process and output).
- Give each participant a printed page for summarizing key actions, decisions, or points to be remembered; an example of such a form follows. Like the earlier example, a blank copy is included in the Appendix, along with permission to reproduce it. Having every participant produce minutes eliminates the need for a secretary or recorder to do so. Each time you reach closure or conclusion on an agenda item, you pause to let participants make note of this on their form.
- If you're conducting a training session, you might distribute a printed page on which participants can respond to questions and learning exercises each time you direct them to the page. An example of such a form is shown in the Appendix.
- On certain questions or issues, participants can respond to their neighbors so that everyone is contributing. People can also be put into subgroups (as described in Chapter 4) to discuss issues and come up with recommendations or conclusions.
- Ask for a show of hands where a variety of opinion is likely to be present: "How many of you feel that . . . ? Let's see hands."
- Have people write down their response to questions or issues that require short answers. Then call on several different participants to share their answers.
- Each of these techniques elicits responses from people you want to contribute. Their response is your opportunity to ask them for more information: for example, why they responded that way or how they knew there was a problem. If you can then reinforce their contribution and make them feel good about sharing it, they will be more likely to participate in the future because you've increased their membership by showing the value of their contribution.

Initiating Action

During the course of a discussion, many actions can help group members achieve their goals—not all of these actions that would have occurred to the group. As the leader, you must initiate such actions. Here are some

MEETING RECAP

Subject: Proposal from Component A
Date of Meeting: Nov. 1
Recap Prepared by: Sharon

Participants: Frank, Tom, Sharon, Chris, Mike

Additional Copies to: Pat

Content Summary: Frank called a meeting of all department supervisors to discuss the proposal submitted by Component A regarding a workload transfer. After a brainstorming session, numerous issues (both pro and con) were identified. Additionally, two possible alternatives to the current proposal were suggested: to outsource all of the work or to transfer only part of the workload to us. It was determined that more information was required and various group members volunteered to obtain the needed data.

Decisions Reached:

None — Additional information is required prior to making a recommendation.

Actions to be Taken	By Whom	When
• Determine specific type and amount work to be transferred	Tom	Nov. 11
• Develop a status report on our department's projected workload and personnel requirements through year end.	Sharon	Nov. 15
• Identify cost of outsourcing the work.	Chris	Nov. 11
• Determine compatibility of equipment	Mike	Nov. 4
• Follow up on above and schedule next meeting	Frank	Nov. 10

examples of situations that suggest the need for you to initiate an action to keep the group moving:

Situation	Suggested Action
Three or four members are actively discussing an issue that other participants are not interested in.	Tell the group that the discussion does not seem to be of interest to the majority (you might want to confirm this), and ask them to continue after your meeting.
Someone has raised an issue that disrupts the flow, yet the participants are interested.	Start a flipchart sheet for topics and issues to be dealt with later—a tickler file.
The issue has come up of how to deal with a certain kind of problem employee (e.g., client, trainee, or customer). You want to get specific and not deal with fuzzy generalities.	Place the person who raised the issue in a spontaneous role play in which you are playing the other role and thus getting a live demonstration of how to deal with the problem.
The group wanted to make a decision today, but now realizes that a key person or critical information is lacking.	Appoint someone to be responsible for bringing the missing person or information to the next meeting.
You realize that the group is coming up with many negatives—reasons a new policy, product, or procedure, will not work. You want them to look at both sides of the issue.	Suggest that we examine all the pros and cons. Place two flipcharts at the front (left and right side), then appoint a recorder for each. Label the charts positives and negatives. Ask the group to brainstorm, listing alternately a pro, a con, a pro, and so on. This flushes out both sides of the issue.
Someone has identified a problem that is hurting the group's productivity (e.g., equipment failure, faulty parts from supplier, or poor service from another department.)	Select a task force to look into the problem and correct it or report at the next meeting on progress and options, thereby avoiding a gripe session.

These examples of initiating action illustrate process actions (i.e., facilitator skills) and do not invade the group's responsibility for the outcome of the meeting. Before you initiate an action, be sure the group is not likely to handle the situation without your intervention. Remember also that there is always a danger of being too forceful and causing the group to resent or even reject the action you want to initiate.

Serving as a Resource

From time to time, members of a group may look to you for your input. If you have knowledge or experience that can help, you may want to share it after making sure that there is no one else in the group who can provide the information the group is looking for.

It's usually best to limit your input to information, avoiding the temptation to give advice or opinion. You want the group to draw on their own members and develop self-reliance rather then discover that they can look to you as a crutch.

The use of questions that lead participants to deduce answers they've asked you for is your greatest value as a resource, because it develops the group's ability to make decisions and solve problems on their own.

For example, suppose you have been leading a group discussion. They've agreed on the likely causes of a problem they are trying to solve, and have just come up with three different ways of dealing with the problem. They now want your advice on which is best. Here are some of the questions you might ask to lead them to select the best course of action:

- What do you see as the pros and cons of each?
- What risk is associated with each? The timetable? The cost?
- Are you equally able to implement all three?

During the course of your questions, they will likely see that one of the three options is best. Although it would have been quicker to have answered their request by giving advice, you have accomplished a much more desirable outcome by not doing so:

- The responsibility for the decision is still theirs—it did not transfer to you.
- They are more committed to a successful implementation of their decision than they might be to yours; they'll work hard to prove they selected the best course of action.
- On future decisions, they can now raise for themselves the questions you've just raised. You've taught them how to evaluate alternatives.

When you're called on to be a resource, you must decide whether your input will advance the group toward its objectives without retarding the group's process skills and ability to function on their own. Questions are your most effective tool to get the group to think things through without depending on the leader for answers.

Structuring

As a leader, you can do many things to set the stage or structure the group for a successful outcome. The items that follow may or may not be appropriate or under your control. But they should be considered.

- *Membership.* Do you have the right members? Will the group function better if someone is added or removed?

- *Physical setting.* Are the room, seating arrangement, and chairs conducive to the purpose of the sessions?
- *Accessories.* Are flipcharts present? Can anyone use them, or only the leader? Are notepads and pencils needed? Is coffee available?
- *Handouts.* Is prework (e.g., a copy of a memo or an article) appropriate? Should data (e.g., tables, graphs, or production figures) be distributed?
- *Assignments.* Should the leader of the group make assignments, form committees, or appoint a task force?
- *Rules.* Is attendance voluntary or mandatory? What happens to members who are often late or absent or are unwilling to serve?

Structuring can be imposed by three sources of authority: the organization, the group itself, and the leader. Before you take up the leadership role of a group, you should clarify the structure of the group and the sources and limits of authority. In some cases, a mission statement or charter can be drafted to clarify issues of structure.

The ultimate source of authority springs from the purpose and goals of the organization. You and your team operate within it. Some types of authority and power may come from the group itself, while other types come from you. In most organizations, some authority overlaps. This is shown in the Venn diagram (Figure 6.1).

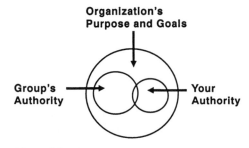

Figure 6.1

As with our earlier discussion of setting limits, a group may impose additional limits and structuring upon itself. This is not likely to happen until the group has functioned for a while and seen a need for it. This is the most desirable source of structuring, of course, and should be recognized as the group's readiness to take responsibility for self-discipline and self-direction.

Handling Problem Participants

Whenever individuals come together to function as a group, differences in personality, perceptions, purpose, and past experience and knowledge usually produce problems. Your role as leader is to deal with these problems without causing the problem participant to lose face or be embarrassed and without disrupting the group process in working toward its goals and objectives.

Problem participants are those who dominate, those who are negative and critical, those who form cliques and pursue their own agendas, those who waste time with personal anecdotes and irrelevancies, and those who overplay the role of comedian. This aspect of your role as leader is important enough to deserve a section dealing with the most common problems and alternative strategies for handling each. Chapter 8 addresses the challenge of how to deal with problem participants.

Summarizing and Follow Up

No meeting should end without devoting the last five minutes or so to a summary that gives closure to the session, identifies the follow-up actions to be taken, and establishes the topic or objectives for the next meeting. Although this can be done by the leader (and often is when the time is running out), the summary is more effective if the participants contribute to it. Here's an example of how that might work:

> "Now, let's wrap it up. We covered four issues today. First, we discussed the problem. Sharon, you played a key role in that discussion. Could you take a minute to summarize the conclusions we came to? (SHARON) Thanks, Sharon. Next, we focused on the need for———. What did we decide there? Who can summarize for us? Yes, Bob. (BOB) And so on."

In our discussion of increasing participation, we explained the idea of having participants keep an ongoing record (or minutes) of decisions reached and follow-up actions to be taken (see meeting recap in the Appendix). If you plan to use this idea, your summary can be handled simply by calling on different participants:

> "Joe, what did you have as the first entry on your sheet? (JOE) Marianne, what was the next entry for follow-up that you noted on your sheet? (MARIANNE) And so on."

Some groups will appoint a recorder to make notes and send out a summary following the meeting. If this is your preference, call on the recorder to give a brief oral report on the decisions reached and follow-up actions and assignments.

You began the meeting by stating the goals and objectives to be accomplished. Your summary should include a return to these objectives to see whether each has been met or whether future action is required to satisfy them.

If your group is a work team and you are their leader, you are probably the one to check with individuals who have assignments and actions to be handled before the next meeting. However, if the group is not one you work with between meetings (e.g., a class that you're facilitating or a committee or task force you're chairing), follow up is more difficult. You might want to set interim checkpoints or one-on-one meetings, perhaps by phone, to make sure that the actions needed before the next meeting are taking place and to see if the participants need help.

Self-Quiz on Roles and Responsibilities

1. What are some of the benefits of putting the goals of a meeting in writing and, whenever possible, sending them to participants in advance?

2. On occasion, a discussion leader must integrate and focus the comments of participants when the discussion is rambling or going astray. Give an example of how you might handle such a situation.

3. A supervisor attending the basics of management course has just made this comment.

    "With all the emphasis on improving our productivity around here, I don't know why you don't send the notebook and course materials out to us at our work places so we could study it on our own and either eliminate or cut down on the time spent in class."

    Indicate how you might rephrase and clarify so as to help the individual and the group understand what is being said.

4. Here are three contributions by participants. In the space below each, indicate how you would deflect and return the comment.

    - I can't see how this new policy applies to our group.

    - You want us to treat our people on an adult-to-adult basis. Yet two of my people are dependent children whom I've got to spoon-feed.

    - Don't talk to me about motivation. We've got a freeze on hiring and on spending, we're downsizing, and push has given way to shove on improving quality and productivity!

5. A participant who is near retirement wants to see employees measuring their weekly output and posting it on the wall as an incentive. A younger participant shoots down the idea with "They need financial incentives, not fancy numbers on the wall." The older man replies with, "Money won't make the difference," which the younger one counters with "That's easy for you to say. Look at the size of your paycheck compared with ours!" How do you relieve the tension?

6. Name several things you can do to set limits and thereby keep activities on target during your meetings.

7. Describe at least five things you might do during a meeting to pick up the level of participation and get everyone responding.

8. What action might you initiate if participants are getting bogged down discussing their frustration with:

    • A new personnel policy that neither you nor they understand?

    • Another department that is not responding to a request for service?

9. When members of the group look to you for advice, why is answering them by asking questions better than telling them what to do?

10. What are some of the issues you should address when establishing the structure and ground rules for your group?

11. Describe the major kinds of problem participants you have come across in meetings you've facilitated.

12. What should you cover during the last few minutes of a meeting to give the session closure?

Making Work Teams Work

The work team and teamwork have been around for centuries. The pyramids, the coliseum, and the great cathedrals are the result of teamwork—the sum of the expended physical effort of thousands of individuals. But when today's work teams expend mental effort in solving problems and making decisions, the result can be more than the sum of the individual contributions. That's the synergy challenge for today's self-directed teams: learning how to make the whole greater than the sum of its parts.

Every manager who has an ounce of pride is likely to be heard saying, "What a great team I've got!" But are they a team? Or merely a group? Are group goals clear and compelling? Do the employees put group goals ahead of individual goals? Do they deal with conflict on a rational, impersonal basis? Do they respect one another's views and input? Do they meet regularly to explore ways of working better?

Learning to function as a team is not an easy lesson. Many people prefer playing singles at tennis—having a partner and playing doubles can be frustrating to a high achiever who doesn't want to be held back by others and may describe teams with terms like *collective incompetence* and *a way of substituting discussion for the dreariness of labor and the loneliness of thought.* That's the high achiever.

The low achiever is comfortable knowing the job and doing things the way they've always been done. Teams are a threat because the members must learn multiple jobs and take on responsibilities that were once reserved for supervisors and managers—hiring, firing, appraising performance, disciplining, and setting schedules. The low achiever feels that management is paid to make those kinds of decisions and that because he or she is not, it shouldn't be his or her job.

In this chapter, we'll examine the factors that are important to the successful growth of self-directed teams (SDTs). A 1992 survey indicated that at least 25% of U.S. organizations have implemented SDTs. We'll examine the four stages of a team's evolution and identify 35 factors that help or hinder the success of SDTs. Specifically, upon completing chapter 7, you should be able to:

- Describe at least three factors that moved companies from pyramidal to matrix organizations.
- Identify the four stages of a team's evolutionary growth.
- Indicate the positive results that can occur during the storming stage.
- Give at least three reasons empowerment takes years in a typical company.
- Rate each of 35 teamwork factors on relevance and effort required.
- Select those factors that have the most impact on your work teams.
- Determine which of five areas have the greatest potential for improved performance of work teams.

In his State of the Union address, the President noted that "The American economy is in trouble. The most resourceful industrialized country on earth ranks among the last in the rate of economic growth. Business investment is on the decline. Profits have fallen. Construction is off. Fewer people are working."

The time was January 1961 and the President was John F. Kennedy. American business was beginning to realize that the three *D*s associated with an organization's rapid growth (decentralization, depersonalization, and delays) were taking their toll on the three *P*s: productivity, personnel, and profit. The big-is-beautiful rule of the first half century seemed to be reaching limits as management realized that the speed of responsiveness to the market, to technology, and to legislation is inversely proportional to the size of an organization. We began to realize that small is beautiful.

For example, Henry Ford developed the new model A in 1927, taking the vehicle from design to delivery in six months. A half-century later, Henry Ford II was producing dozens of models with an average development time of 5 to 6 years. Decentralization and depersonalization accompanied the growing delays in lead time from concept to customer. Clearly, the U.S. was facing productivity problems.

One solution was to move from a hierarchical organization chart like that shown in Figure 7.1 to a matrix organization in which employees serve on teams that are created and dissolved as determined by ever-changing needs and opportunities. The bureaucratic organization was rapidly becoming a dysfunctional dinosaur, threatened with extinction. Through a series of reorganizations and transformations, teams began to emerge as a new way of doing business, and a matrix style of manage-

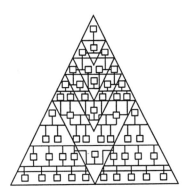
Traditional Organization

Figure 7.1

ment replaced the autocratic style that had been alive and well for centuries (see Figure 7.2)

In 1965, Bruce Tuckman introduced a model that identified the four stages of growth that a team typically experiences: forming, norming, storming, and performing. By understanding the dynamics and characteristics of each stage, team members and their leaders can recognize and accept the evolutionary cycle and minimize the less productive stages so as to reach maturity and full productivity as rapidly as possible.

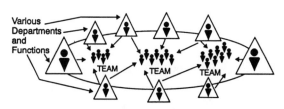
Matrix Organization

Figure 7.2

Although Tuckman's four stages apply to many types of group activity, they are most relevant to the formation of self-directed teams. (We've been using the more traditional types of teams for many years: task force, project group, cross-functional teams, supervised work unit, and so on.) The self-directed team has less supervision and more autonomy, and requires an in-depth understanding of the four stages if it is to survive. The following sections describe each of the four stages.

Forming

During this stage, members clarify their mission: what must be done, by whom, what goals and objectives must be met, and by when. This is the task-oriented side of forming. As for the people-oriented side, members voice their concerns about a number of issues:

- What effect will my membership have on my career (e.g., growth, salary, or promotability)? Will team achievement or personal accomplishments be the basis of my appraisals? Do I now have more or less control over my performance? Who is my boss?
- What roles will I fill on the team? How will others perceive me? Accept me? What can we learn from one another? Can I trust them? What rewards and what rules go with membership on this team?
- What kind of leadership do we have? What authority? How will I relate to the leader? Do we have the right skills and experience to get the job done? What changes will occur? How permanent is the team? What will happen thereafter?

Norming

As the name suggests, members establish the norms for working together. Expectations, standards, and policies and procedures are set in response to member needs (i.e., the questions raised under forming) and to organizational needs (i.e., the reason for creating the team). These are the task-oriented issues that must be addressed during norming.

On the people-oriented side, members need to resolve operational concerns relating to the interpersonal dynamics of the group. By this stage, they have worked together as a group long enough to know what norms will convert the group into a team with minimal time and maximal satisfaction. These norms cluster around three major issues: leadership, membership, and processes.

- Leadership. Is the leader a boss or coach? Will the team be self-governed or supervisor-led? What degree of structure, authority, and expertise is required by members? Is the leader a linking pin with other teams and management? What authority does the leader have over members requiring discipline? Is leadership rotated? Under what terms and conditions? Should the team have multiple leaders who serve simultaneously and are responsible for different aspects of the team's operations?
- Membership. What are the prerequisites for membership? What responsibilities do members have toward one another (e.g., in giving feedback, mentoring, developing trust, appraising performance, or dealing with unacceptable behavior)? What process will be followed in acquiring a

new member or getting rid of an unacceptable one? What time demands are appropriate to expect of members? What are the plans for training and developing team members (both as a group and for personal growth)?
- Processes. How will the team: Solve problems? Make decisions (e.g., will it be consensus or majority vote or decision matrix or outside expertise)? Maintain links with other teams? Conduct meetings? Record minutes and actions to be taken? Give assignments? Develop facilitation skills? Calculate costs and benefits? Measure and maintain quality? Communicate both within and outside the team? Move from parent-to-child relationships to adult-to-adult relationships?

Storming

Whenever people must work together, differences in perceptions, personalities, purpose, and past experience inevitably create conflict. However, this also has a desirable effect: members become aroused, interested, and more likely to get deeply involved than to treat an issue superficially. Achievers are competitive and confident, and typically thrive in an atmosphere of conflict.

The issue is therefore not whether conflict can be eliminated but how it can be controlled so that it releases energy rather than draining it. Here are some of the questions that should be addressed so that storming remains in check and serves as a constructive force:

- Who will control conflict? Who are the referees that can blow the whistle and freeze the action?
- Is it appropriate to establish a cooling off period before a hot issue can be addressed again?
- What types of conflict are likely to arise, both internally and with other teams or management? (Forewarned is forearmed.)
- What issues are non-negotiable and are thus banned from team discussion (e.g., departmental politics, union contracts, or gossip)?
- What is the process by which members bring up a complaint, grievance, or conflict? Are there neutral arbitrators available?

Performing

Although the prior three stages of development seem necessary in the evolutionary cycle of a team, they do not add direct value to the products and services the team must deliver. Therefore, the time spent getting to the fourth stage, performing, should be controlled so that productivity—

a high output of quality work at manageable costs—is reached as soon as possible.

In the past, functions such as quality assurance, safety, and methods improvement were left to staff specialists. Today's teams can be viewed as mini corporations taking on the responsibility for all activities that affect their performance. This means that ongoing training is needed as members learn the concepts and skills needed to manage their new responsibilities: SPC (statistical process control), TQM (total quality management), continuous improvement process, and benchmarking.

Three major categories of issues and questions must be addressed during the performing stage:

- Measurement. How will we track performance? Quantify output? Measure errors and defects? Can these measures be converted into dollars to produce a profit-and-loss statement for the team? How frequently should we post the score (weekly, monthly, or quarterly)?
- Improvement. What level of productivity (output over input) have we achieved? How much further can we push it without experiencing negative side effects? When do we need technical expertise, and where do we get it? What authority do we have to stop production until a quality problem is corrected?
- Personnel. What growth and mobility can team members expect? How do we deal with turnover? Do team members interview new candidates for membership? Are performance appraisals done by the group? How is the discipline of nonconforming members handled?

When the Party Is Over

Teams are created to fill many needs: special projects, new product development, manufacture of a certain model or component, improvement of service, and so on. All of these needs have a life cycle, and the team's mission eventually comes to an end. This might mean disbanding the team, assigning a new mission, or scaling down and reassigning members to other teams. This is always painful when the team has evolved together and reached a high level of productivity.

Some organizations believe in dealing with this when it occurs. Others prefer to prepare members well in advance of the inevitable, and involve them in exploring alternative strategies. When a team changes the composition of its members, the four-stage cycle often must begin again with forming. But the process of evolution is much quicker now because established members have developed teamwork skills and a commitment to reach the performing stage as soon as possible.

In healthy organizations that can weather the storms of recession, downsizing, and stagnant markets, teams are a way of responding to adversity, and the life cycle repeats itself as new teams are launched. But such firms may be the exception rather than the rule. In most organizations, employees are dubious and skeptical of the new doctrine of empowerment.

Management support is often missing during the first and second stages of a team's life cycle. Senior managers are concerned for their own role and future. They may fear that someone has unlocked the cell blocks and that the inmates are trying to run the asylum. Their relationships at work, at home, and with customers and such stakeholders as suppliers and distributors are still conducted on a parent-to-child basis. The transition to adult-to-adult relationships is threatened by their insecurity. In fact, at the very time that adult-to-adult relationships are needed if TQM and work teams are to be effective, the uncertainty surrounding motives and outcomes felt by all employees is bringing out parent-to-child behavior and in some organizations widening the gap between management and workers.

If work teams are to mature and pass through their four stages of growth, the culture of the organization must change. Empowered workers and managers must understand the dynamics of change; they must realize that they are both on board the same ship. Like other huge ships, the organization:

- Has been going the same direction (parent-to-child) for many years. This direction has been appropriate in the past, but is less and less so now.
- Takes a long time to turn (circular, not linear).
- Should experience business as usual during the turn (since a stopped ship can't turn). Everyone on board (from bridge to boiler room) will be frustrated by the slowness and by the seeming lack of progress (the turning radius of a ship is often so big that it may still appear to be going straight).

At the risk of simplifying the enormously challenging and complex task of overhauling an organization's way of relating to all its stakeholders, I suggest that the process must begin with top management, must work its way down the organizational chart, and must assess and then systematically develop the values, styles, qualities, and beliefs needed by all employees if the organization is going to make the successful transition to empowerment.

Too many organizations have launched workshops on TQM, employee involvement, SPC, self-directed teams, and continuous improvement with a heavy focus on imparting knowledge and skills, but with little if any attention to attitude—that is, the values, styles, qualities, and beliefs that facilitate the application of new knowledge and skills.

Moreover, the training is usually given to work groups with little if any attention given to whether management has been to workshops dealing with the actions needed to empower a team, to move from parent to adult, and to facilitate rather than block the organization's move to empowerment.

The list that follows contains 35 key issues that work teams have had to address. Your ability to recognize them and to deal with them effectively strengthens your team-building efforts. They are listed under five headings, with seven key issues under each. Here are the five headings:

- Organizational behavior.
- Supervision and management.
- Membership and leadership.
- Training and development.
- Goals and responsibilities.

We've included a rating system that will help you to identify the priorities and areas of greatest opportunity in developing your team. You'll be rating each of the 35 issues on two factors: its relevance to the success of your team and the amount of effort required to implement the idea (or to undo or rework a false start). Relevance refers to the importance or applicability or appropriateness of the issue or idea. Don't be concerned with whether you are using the idea now. Instead, think about whether it applies and is relevant or worthy of consideration. Effort required refers to the amount of time and energy needed to get an issue or idea accepted and implemented. If it's already in place and working, a rating of low or none should be your response.

Organizational Behavior

Ratings: 3—high   2—moderate   1—low   0—none

1. Managers and workers must each learn to discard old roles and adopt new ones. Managers must discard their traditional parent role (judgmental or nurturing, Hard X or Soft X). Workers must be weaned from their traditional child role of dependency and Not OK feelings. Both groups must become adult-to-adult at the same time. Many organizations have created problems by teaching team building and empowerment to one group first, then the other.

   Relevancy: ☐   **Effort required:** ☐

2. Empowerment is evolutionary, not revolutionary. It works best when done gradually, one department or function at a time—quietly and without fanfare and drama. Major announcements and speeches create suspicion and distrust. Start slowly and win some modest victories. Use your initial work teams as a laboratory in which you can control,

experiment, and refine until you know what does and doesn't work. Then you are ready to enlarge the movement.

Relevancy: ☐   **Effort required:** ☐

3. As employees gain the confidence and competency to assume more self-direction in their work teams, managers must gain the tolerance and trust to step back. They must learn to trade in their old sources of power (rank, position, or control) for the new sources of power (influencing, mentoring, and empowering). This give and take must be orchestrated to occur simultaneously—a bit like Newton's third law: for every action, there's an equal and opposite reaction.

Relevancy: ☐   **Effort required:** ☐

4. Americans are impatient, yet the experts (Peter Drucker, Rensis Likert, George Odiorne) tell us that it takes three to five years to implement any major changes in the way an organization functions. Do managers and workers have the patience to see empowerment through the false starts and second doubts. Or will they join the doubting Thomases: "I knew this wouldn't work," or "I've been here 22 years and seen similar things come and go." Be prepared to invest five years in making empowerment work.

Relevancy: ☐   **Effort required:** ☐

5. What worked at XYZ Company may not work for you or may not even be appropriate for you. Following NBC's two-hour special, "If Japan Can, Why Can't We?", hundreds of teams of U.S. managers and technicians visited Japan's highly publicized companies and attempted to copy them, often with unhappy results. Companies, like countries, have their own cultures. And cross-cultural translations are tricky. Although we can and should learn from the successes and failures of others, every organization must be prepared to write its own history of team building.

Relevancy: ☐   **Effort required:** ☐

6. If team building is to spread throughout your organization, you may wish to overstaff your initial teams so that you can spin off key members after the team is running smoothly and use them to begin new

teams. An analogy is appropriate: in making sourdough bread, buttermilk, or yogurt, it's a good idea to set aside a portion of the original batch and earmark it as the culture to be used in starting future batches.

Relevancy: ☐   **Effort required:** ☐

7. With the spread of teams, policies and reward structures must change. For example, incentives like cash awards for employee suggestions might have to be changed to reward team improvements rather than (or as well as) individual initiative. Similarly, if the production line work team in a bottling plant is able to meet its quota by the end of Thursday, they may have earned a three-day weekend. Flextime, job enlargement (horizontal loading), job enrichment (vertical loading), the four-day workweek, profit sharing, and equity sharing are helping to maintain team enthusiasm after the initial excitement is over.

Relevancy: ☐   **Effort required:** ☐

Your reactions to these seven key issues:

Relevancy (sum of your seven ratings) ☐

Effort Required (sum of your seven ratings) ☐

Sum of these Two Boxes ☐

Which ideas, if any, have you selected to share with others and decide how best to implement? (Refer to ideas by number) _____ .

What barriers, if any, might make it difficult for you to put into practice the ideas you selected?

Supervision and Management

Ratings: 3—high   2—moderate   1—low   0—none

8. A newly-organized work team is not likely to be self-directed for a year or so. Change is invariably accompanied by uncertainty and depend-

ency. Supervisors and managers should expect to be coaches, mentors, and resources, providing structure and direction during a team's formative period. The adjectives *self-directed, autonomous,* and *independent* may create unrealistic expectations. Team members and their leaders must be developed. Team members must be weaned from their dependency on close supervision. Supervisors haven't been re-placed, they've been re-placed into new roles as facilitators.

Relevancy: ☐   **Effort required:** ☐

9. No less dangerous than the abdicators are those managers who pay lip service to employee involvement and empowerment because it's the current party line. Employees have their doubts and will attach more credibility to management if everyone enters the team-building program with an open mind, acknowledging the doubts, roadblocks, and pitfalls as well as the benefits and potential victories. The organization needs champions, not zealots.

Relevancy: ☐   **Effort required:** ☐

10. To fill their roles as facilitators of the empowerment process, supervisors and managers need feedback from team members on where their actions are supportive of teamwork and where they might be impeding or frustrating the team's efforts. The climate must encourage a team to give managers feedback aimed at improving the relationship. And tools should be made available (surveys, focus sessions, or inventories) for collecting this feedback.

Relevancy: ☐   **Effort required:** ☐

11. The role of first-line supervisors will change during empowerment, causing uncertainty and insecurity in the very people who are the key to making work teams work. They should be involved in the program design, on the steering committees, and in the training and development of the teams. They need a clear picture of their new roles in advance. They should also be assured that there's no hidden agenda, that the success of their teams depends on their coaching skills, and that they will still have jobs.

Relevancy: ☐   **Effort required:** ☐

12. Managers should model the behavior that they expect of team members—that is, to ask questions, to trust, to be positive and supportive, to listen openly to the suggestions and opinions of others, to summarize to confirm understanding, to think *we* rather than *me*, and so on. Actions speak louder than words, and a manager's own behavior should be a model of teamwork. The parent-child relationships of yesterday must become the adult-adult relationships of effective work teams.

   Relevancy: ☐   **Effort required:** ☐

13. Supervisors and managers must continue to be guardians of the interests of stockholders and owners, enforcing policy and procedures, ensuring that contractual commitments are honored, aligning organizational resources with team needs, setting goals and expectations, and serving as referees and judges on questions regarding the acceptability of actions being proposed or engaged in by work teams. Although empowerment means that responsibility is moved down the organization chart, many decisions and functions must remain the prerogative of management. A clear understanding of the division of authority and responsibility between management and work teams is important to the success of any program of empowerment.

   Relevancy: ☐   **Effort required:** ☐

14. In an empowered organization, the span of control for supervisors and managers often increases as teams become more self-directed over time. This means that a manager may be responsible for several teams—more people than they may have supervised in the traditional hierarchical organization. Managers who once served as vertical linking pins are now horizontal links, coordinating the goals and activities of related, interdependent work teams.

   Relevancy: ☐   **Effort required:** ☐

Your reactions to these seven key issues:

Relevancy (sum of your seven ratings)   ☐

Effort Required (sum of your seven ratings)   ☐

Sum of these Two Boxes   ☐

Which ideas, if any, have you selected to share with others and decide how best to implement? (Refer to ideas by number) _____ .

What barriers, if any, might make it difficult for you to put into practice the ideas you selected?

Membership and Leadership

Ratings: 3—high   2—moderate   1—low   0—none

15. Empowerment isn't for everyone. Many employees do not want any more responsibility or power than they already have. They've got a good job, a regular paycheck, and are happy with things as they are. They would rather take their orders from management than have their peers solving problems and making suggestions in work teams. At least a quarter of the employees in most organizations fall into this category, and they may hamper your efforts at team work and empowerment.

    Relevancy: ☐   **Effort required:** ☐

16. If teams are to develop leaders, guidelines should be established to help this process. For example, the position of team leader might be held for a term of, say, six months or one year, with only one reelection allowed. Another example is to have two team leaders: the content leader (concerned with tasks and what gets done) and the process leader (concerned with relationships and how the team and its members function). Another example is to have different members heading the 3 to 4 person project teams, ad hoc committees, and task forces that must be formed from time to time.

    Relevancy: ☐   **Effort required:** ☐

17. Team leaders must also function as team members. They should have the same responsibilities and duties as other team members. They should receive training (and perhaps all members should) in group facilitation skills and should function as facilitators and not as super-

visors. They serve as the bridge, or linking pin, between the team and management, but they should receive no special privileges or status that might separate them from their fellow team members.

Relevancy: ☐   **Effort required:** ☐

18. The steering committees that oversee the formation and integration of work teams should include members who represent a broad slice of the organization, both vertically (many levels of authority) and horizontally (many functions and departments). In addition to representing a variety of job skills, they should be open, frank, outspoken, and committed to doing what's best for the organization (rather than representing their constituency).

Relevancy: ☐   **Effort required:** ☐

19. Work teams should meet from time to time with other work teams whose functions are contingent or interdependent. It may also be appropriate for a team to have one or two of its members serving on another team—that is, interlocking membership when the input and output of team meetings should not be restricted to the activities of one team. Obviously the degree to which linking members is appropriate depends on the structure of the organization and the nature of the work flow.

Relevancy: ☐   **Effort required:** ☐

20. Teams should be given tools (e.g., surveys, checklists, or group exercises) that will enable them to periodically examine and modify their roles, rules, relationships, and responsibilities—this is the process side of how well they are functioning. These tools might also include learning exercises that strengthen their skills in working together effectively.

Relevancy: ☐   **Effort required:** ☐

21. Team meetings should be summarized in minutes that give recap (actions and decisions), recognition (who has done what), and reminders (who will do what before the next meeting). These minutes should go to each member, to management, to the leaders of related

work teams, and perhaps to the steering committee. The role of the recorder who generates the minutes might be rotated.

Relevancy: ☐   **Effort required:** ☐

Your reactions to these seven key issues:

Relevancy (sum of your seven ratings)   ☐

Effort Required (sum of your seven ratings)   ☐

Sum of these Two Boxes   ☐

Which ideas, if any, have you selected to share with others and decide how best to implement? (Refer to ideas by number) _____ .

What barriers, if any, might make it difficult for you to put into practice the ideas you selected?

Training and Development

Ratings: 3—high   2—moderate   1—low   0—none

22. As teams are organized, their members should be trained in the functions that were previously handled by management: how to solve problems, monitor quality, make decisions, conduct meetings, resolve conflict, and so on. Many training exercises are available. Team-building workshops are useful in the initial stages of formation, and developmental sessions should be planned on an ongoing basis (typically one per month).

    Relevancy: ☐   **Effort required:** ☐

23. When times are uncertain, employees may revert to a child state of dependency on management. The danger is that managers may abdicate (You bought the farm, now run it) or be overly participative (What do you all think?). Empowerment and employee involvement do not mean that the work teams are running the organization. Man-

agement must give direction and be directive when this is required. Managers and team members should be trained in their respective roles, responsibilities, and areas of freedom.

Relevancy: ☐   **Effort required:** ☐

24. Team development follows an up and down progress chart. Growth is not smooth and linear. The stages of development (forming, storming, norming, and performing) should be recognized and dealt with as a team moves along the continuum from strong dependency on supervision and coaching to self-direction and greater autonomy. Members should be taught how to deal with the bumps and curves in the road.

Relevancy: ☐   **Effort required:** ☐

25. Case studies, articles, and visits to other teams are useful learning exercises. So are games and simulations that foster cooperation and shared perceptions (e.g., survival games or construction simulations). Because their success depends heavily on facilitation skills and discovery learning, experienced HRD instructors are probably the persons in the best position to conduct such training.

Relevancy: ☐   **Effort required:** ☐

26. In organizations in which compensation is geared to one's knowledge, skill level, or productivity, training should be modular and competency based, with each achievement level requiring certification and approval based on one's performance on tests that measure application rather than acquisition (simulations and what-if situations).

Relevancy: ☐   **Effort required:** ☐

27. No two team members will display the same level of skills on the competencies required to do the job. The buddy system is an excellent way to upgrade performance. Create pairs that consist of high and low performers; the more skilled one is responsible for coaching and mentoring. Such pairs can be created and dissolved frequently, so that each team member is a mentor and coach to others in some area of strength.

Relevancy: ☐   **Effort required:** ☐

28. During the awareness training that occurs at the start of an empowerment program, all parties (stakeholders) should share the same message, mission, and master plan: Why we're going this way, what we should and shouldn't expect, and how we'll proceed. Mixed groups of workers, supervisors, and managers should be scheduled to receive this orientation at the same time (regardless of when their functional area is scheduled to be formed into work teams).

Relevancy: ☐   **Effort required:** ☐

Your reactions to these seven key issues:

Relevancy (sum of your seven ratings) ☐

Effort Required (sum of your seven ratings) ☐

Sum of these Two Boxes ☐

Which ideas, if any, have you selected to share with others and decide how best to implement? (Refer to ideas by number) _____ .

What barriers, if any, might make it difficult for you to put into practice the ideas you selected?

Goals and Responsibilities

Ratings: 3—high   2—moderate   1—low   0—none

29. The goals and expectations of each team should be short-term (weekly or monthly), so that the team can experience frequent victories and celebrate major ones. Nothing succeeds like success. Many teams post their goals (quotas or tolerances) on the wall at the start of the week or month, then add the actual figures obtained. Like any team sport, there's much more excitement and effort when the score is posted with each small gain.

Relevancy: ☐   **Effort required:** ☐

30. Whenever possible, new teams should start with easier goals and progress to more difficult ones. Decisions and actions can be arranged in rank order from simpler to more complex. Initially management can handle more complex issues, but the thinking and procedure followed should be shared with the team to prepare members for handling such decisions and actions in the future.

Relevancy: ☐   **Effort required:** ☐

31. Job satisfaction is much greater in goal-oriented work teams. If the work is routine and quality is already as high as it is likely to get, the group may need outside goals to keep them challenged and committed, for example: community service, plant beautification, adopting a youth group, winning a softball league competition, preserving the environment, and so on. Some organizations release people during work time for such projects when production quotas have been met.

Relevancy: ☐   **Effort required:** ☐

32. Many goals for growth and personal improvement are related to the meetings the teams hold. There are goals to improve clarity of objectives, group time management, quality of reports by committees and task forces, conciseness of minutes taken, control of digressions, and so on. Each meeting might end with a five-minute critique of where the group succeeded and failed in achieving the goals of running an effective meeting.

Relevancy: ☐   **Effort required:** ☐

33. A major goal of every sports team is to have high-performing players. When this does not happen, a player's contract is not renewed, or he is traded to another team that provides a better match. Work teams need to agree on the goals, expectations, and performance criteria of all members and to have a procedure, understood by all, for removing a member who is not contributing to the team's effectiveness.

Relevancy: ☐   **Effort required:** ☐

34. Not all organizational functions lend themselves to teams. For example, although a divisional sales manager might be fond of bragging about his or her team of top-performing salespeople, the salespeople are in fact often in competition and may have little if any incentive to cooperate with one another. Nor do they function as a group—each has certain accounts or territories and manages them independent of the others. Teams should not be formed where the work does not lend itself to work groups.

   Relevancy: ☐ **Effort required:** ☐

35. The ultimate goal of teams is improved productivity, quality, and customer satisfaction. Suppose your teams achieve a 20% increase in output. If the market hasn't also grown by 20%, the price of all this improved performance is that fewer people are needed to meet the demand. The result will be layoffs and a reduction in force. Management should discuss with workers the consequences of better productivity, because it is on the minds of employees as work teams discuss security—their own as well as the organization's.

   Relevancy: ☐ **Effort required:** ☐

Your reactions to these seven key issues:

Relevancy (sum of your seven ratings) ☐

Effort Required (sum of your seven ratings) ☐

Sum of these Two Boxes ☐

Which ideas, if any, have you selected to share with others and decide how best to implement? (Refer to ideas by number) _____ .

What barriers, if any, might make it difficult for you to put into practice the ideas you selected?

Self-Quiz on Making Teams Work

It's now time to total your ratings and see what they mean. Enter the sums in the boxes provided:

Organizational Behavior
Sum of the seven relevancy ratings ☐

Sum of the seven effort required ratings ☐

Sum of these two boxes ☐

Supervision and Management
Sum of the seven relevancy ratings ☐

Sum of the seven effort required ratings ☐

Sum of these two boxes ☐

Membership and Leadership
Sum of the seven relevancy ratings ☐

Sum of the seven effort required ratings ☐

Sum of these two boxes ☐

Training and Development
Sum of the seven relevancy ratings ☐

Sum of the seven effort required ratings ☐

Sum of these two boxes ☐

Goals and Responsibilities
Sum of the seven relevancy ratings ☐

Sum of the seven effort required ratings ☐

Sum of these two boxes ☐

Sum of the five box scores on relevancy ☐

Sum of the five box scores on effort required ☐

Sum of both of the above boxes (Total Score) ☐

Interpreting Your Responses

1. Look at your total on relevancy. The highest score possible is 105. A score of less than 60 indicates that your organization's approach to team building and empowerment is probably different in nature from that of many other organizations. The higher your score, the greater the uses to which you can put this list. If the relevancy total is greater than the effort required by more than 30 points, you probably have a very supportive and empowered organization.
2. Look at your total on effort required box score. Again, the highest score possible is 105. The higher your score, the more time and energy is needed to carry out the suggestions in our list of 35 issues. If the effort required total is greater than the relevancy total by more than 20 points, it probably is not worth the effort to implement the suggestions.
3. Look at your total score box. The highest possible score is 210. Any score higher than 140 indicates that you have many opportunities but a long way to go in bringing work teams and empowerment to maturity.
4. Compare the box scores on each of the five areas. Are certain topics and activities more relevant than others? Should these be the areas to focus on first? Will they provide the greatest impact on the success of your team building efforts?
5. Compare the box scores on effort required on each of the five areas. Will certain areas require more effort to implement than others? What are your priorities?
6. The need is greatest where relevancy and effort required are both high. Compare the scores in the five areas (i.e., the sum of the two boxes). This can help you select the areas that have the greatest potential for improving your team building program.
7. Similarly, within each area, the need and opportunity are greatest on those items where the two scores add up to a sum of 5 or 6.
8. What actions and priorities do you see as appropriate based on your ratings of these 35 issues? Should team members go through this exercise and discuss the issues? Or is this the role of the steering committee or management?

8

Meeting Leadership

Meetings are a forum for shared thinking. Sometimes the flow of facts and feelings is largely vertical and one-way, from leader to group, as in a military briefing, church sermon, college lecture, after-dinner speaker, or political rally. However, in an empowered organization, the flow is horizontal and two-way, as members exchange facts and feelings, solve problems, make decisions, and work toward consensus.

The societies of ancient Greece and Rome believed in open assembly and discussion as the best way to solve problems and win public acceptance. In New England, town meetings and crackerbarrel discussions at the general store became the backbone of the democratic process. Today's self-directed teams have their roots in the thinking of such pioneers as Mary Parker Follett. In 1918, her writings advocated group meetings in which workers could "integrate" their differences, using "conference as the method" for exercising their "pluralistic responsibility." She believed that compromises leave everyone less than satisfied, and majority rule leaves in its wake an uncooperative minority, ready to undermine any gains.

Studies of learning have demonstrated many times over that lectures may be effective for imparting information, but no method surpasses small group discussion for winning commitment and producing action. When a meeting is facilitated effectively, the interaction is dynamic. It generates power that can be harnessed and channeled into high levels of quality output and productivity.

In this chapter, you'll learn some of the tools and techniques for running a meeting effectively: setting appropriate objectives, defining roles and responsibilities, balancing process and content, dealing with problem participants, and setting the contract (i.e., the ground rules and expectations). Specifically, upon completion of chapter 8, you should be able to:

- Prepare meeting objectives that satisfy three conditions.
- Apply eight criteria in evaluating the quality of your objectives.
- Describe the four roles and responsibilities filled by meeting participants.
- State four precautions a facilitator should take to make meetings more successful.
- Describe the general procedure for dealing with any problem participant.
- Explain how you would deal with a negative, hostile participant.
- List five guidelines or ground rules for dealing with any problem participant.
- Illustrate with four examples what a set of meeting guidelines (ground rules) might look like.
- Prepare a set of guidelines that are appropriate for the meetings you facilitate.

Preparing Objectives

Every meeting should begin with a statement of the objectives. Where a meeting notice is appropriate, the objectives should be spelled out in advance of the meeting. Participants need to know the answers to several important questions: Why are we here? Is this meeting going to make good use of my time? What input or output is expected of me? How can I affect or be affected by the results of this meeting?

The key word in any statement of objectives is the verb. In a results-oriented objective, the verb spells out the desired outcome. It leaves no doubt in the minds of participants as to whether or not the meeting achieved its purpose. Let's look at an example of a results-oriented objective of one work team:

> To identify the likely causes of increased absenteeism on Monday, to generate a half-dozen alternative strategies for correcting it, and to decide on a plan of action that should reduce by 30% the current rate over the next three months.

There are four verb forms in this objective: to identify, to generate, to decide, and should reduce. These are results-oriented verbs that enable participants and the leader to run a successful meeting.

All too often, however, the objectives of a meeting are not stated in the form of outcomes. The verb may describe an activity (process) or a wish. For example, sloppier versions of our objective on absenteeism might look like this:

> To discuss the problem of high absenteeism on Mondays.
> To correct the unacceptably high Monday absenteeism.

In the first statement, the verb (to discuss) describes an activity or process. How will the group know when they have discussed it? The problem with activity verbs is that they have no end—the group could discuss absenteeism for two minutes or two hours. Nor is there any way of knowing whether their discussion was relevant, because there is no indication of the outcome that should result from all that discussion.

In the second statement, the verb (to correct) describes a wish. How will the group know when they have corrected it? Suppose that over the next three months, Monday absenteeism goes down by one percent. Will they have corrected it? How about five percent? Is this enough correction? Again, there is no indication of outcome that is clear enough to help the group to act appropriately at the meeting and enable the group to evaluate the success of the outcome. A well-prepared objective meets both these criteria.

There's a third criteria that objectives should meet: the verb must describe a behavior that is appropriate to the group. Again, let's illustrate this with sloppier versions of the absenteeism objective:

To write a new policy on Monday absenteeism.
To approve a new policy to deal with Monday absenteeism on a companywide basis.

Both of these statements violate the criteria of appropriateness. The first verb (to write) is not an appropriate use of group time—writing is an individual activity. One person should write the policy, then bring it to the meeting. The group might want to edit, modify, or to adapt. These are appropriate group activities; writing is not.

The second statement tells us that the department head plans to approve a new companywide policy. It is not likely that any one department can approve a policy for the whole company. Objectives must not state outcomes that lie outside the charter or authority of the group.

The criteria we've been discussing can be applied—as a checklist—to make sure that your meeting objectives are effective:

1. The verb should spell out the desired outcomes of the actions taken at the meeting or as a result of the meeting.
2. These results-oriented verbs should describe measurable, observable outcomes (e.g., to decide which of the three methods we should implement, to set up a plan for dealing with the problem of shrinkage, or to cut $12,000 from next year's proposed budget).
3. The objective should avoid verbs that describe activities (e.g., to discuss, to look into, to examine, or to report), because these are processes and could go on indefinitely. If you do list them, make sure they are followed by an objective that is results-oriented and shows why the activity will take place; for example: to hear the consultant's recommendations and decide which course of action to implement. In this case, to hear is an activity, but the reason is immediately clear.

4. The objective should avoid verbs that describe wishes (e.g., to strengthen our relations with unit C, to reduce accidents, or to improve productivity). The problem here is in knowing how to measure the outcome.
5. The objective should be stated in terms that are explicit enough (clear, detailed, and crisp) to help the meeting participants stay on target and minimize discussion that does not contribute directly to their attainment of the objective.
6. When possible, the objective should enable participants to evaluate the degree of success they have or haven't achieved in implementing the actions agreed upon at the meeting.
7. The objective should be limited to actions that make appropriate use of group time. To write a first draft is not a group activity. Neither is to read the consultant's report. Both should be done by participants working individually before the meeting.
8. The objective should not exceed the charter or authority of the group. If an objective requires the authority of a ranking member who does not show up, it should be set aside until the person is present.

Defining Roles and Responsibilities

Confusion over roles and responsibilities is a common meeting problem. Very often, participants are not clear who is supposed to be doing what. In the book, *How to Make Meetings Work* (New York. Jove Publishing, 1986), Michael Doyle and David Straus suggest four well-defined roles and responsibilities that together form a self-correcting system of checks and balances to keep a meeting on track. All four roles are equally important. Each contributes to the health and productivity of a group. Everyone has a stake in the outcome and is equally responsible for the success or failure of the group. They call their system the Interaction Method. The four roles are:

- *The facilitator.* The responsibility of the facilitator is to help the group focus on its task by suggesting methods and procedures, protecting all members of the group from attack, and making sure everyone has an opportunity to participate. The facilitator does not evaluate or contribute ideas. The facilitator is also responsible for premeeting and postmeeting logistics.
- *The recorder.* The responsibility of the recorder is to write down basic ideas on large sheets of paper (flipcharts) in front of the participants. The objective is to capture enough of what is said so that ideas can be preserved and recalled at any time. Participants know that their contributions have been heard and preserved in full view of the group. The recorder does not evaluate or contribute ideas either.
- *The group member.* The group member is an active participant in the

meeting. The control of what happens rests in the hands of the group members. They can make procedural suggestions, overrule the suggestions of the facilitator, and generally determine the course of the meeting. Beyond that, group members devote all of their energies to the task. It is the responsibility of the group member to keep the facilitator and the recorder in their roles and to make sure ideas are recorded accurately.
- *The manager or chairperson.* The manager or chairperson does not run the meeting but becomes an active participant. Otherwise, he or she retains all other powers and responsibilities. The manager makes all final decisions; sets organizational and personal constraints; regains control, if not satisfied with the progress of the meeting; sets the agenda; argues actively for his or her points of view; urges group members to accept tasks and deadlines; and represents the group in meetings with other groups.

In traditional work groups, the manager or chairperson is present to ensure that the authority is available to approve or veto the group's recommendations. However, in an empowered organization, self-directed teams have the authority for certain actions, and must forward recommendations to a steering committee for other types of actions. Therefore, the manager or chairperson is often not present in these meetings.

For meetings to be effective:

- Roles and responsibilities must be clearly defined and agreed upon.
- The objectives and agenda should be made known to all participants by the facilitator at the start of the meeting, if not beforehand. (See the suggested form in the Appendix.)
- Everyone present should have reasons and opportunities to participate. When people do not contribute, questions arise: Why were they present? Should they attend future meetings? Could the facilitator have gotten them involved?
- The outcomes (decisions, agreement on actions, assignments, etc.) should be recorded and distributed to assure follow-up and continuity.

Balancing Process and Content

In their classic book, *The Managerial Grid* (Houston: Gulf, 1964), Robert Blake and Jane Mouton point out that supervisors and managers must perform a constant balancing act between productivity concerns (the task) and relationship concerns (the people). Similarly, instructors are taught to deal simultaneously with course content and teaching method, and salespeople are taught to blend their product knowledge with their ability to draw out customers and get them involved in the sale.

These three examples illustrate a common problem: confusion of content and process. It is especially obvious at meetings. Participants are often unclear as to whether they are talking about how to discuss a topic or what topic to discuss. It's common for members of a group to plunge into a problem or decision or new topic without reaching agreement on how to proceed and how to know when they've met the objective of their discussion.

Content is concerned with what—what will be discussed, what problems will be solved, what decisions will be dealt with, what goals will be set, and so on. In contrast, process is concerned with how—how the issues will be presented and resolved, how the agenda will be handled, how the participants will be involved, how decisions will be made, and so on.

Content includes the problems, topics, issues (facts and feelings), and agenda items that are being considered. Process includes the approach, the methods, and the procedures to be used in working on the problems, topics, or agenda items.

In problem solving, for example, the content includes evidence, symptoms, suspected causes, alternative actions, criteria of acceptability, and so on. The process is the method by which the group plans to identify and solve the problem—for example, the seven- or eight-step approaches commonly taught in problem-solving courses. For example:

- If gum is the content, chewing may be the process.
- If topic is the content, lecturing may be the process.
- If ball is the content, hitting may be the process.
- If plan is the content, presenting may be the process.
- If problem is the content, defining may be the process.

In short, success in conducting meetings effectively depends on a degree of skill from leader and participants alike in distinguishing between content and process, in dealing with both of them simultaneously and in not letting heavy content input (information dumping) overshadow the group's ability to process the content.

Although the facilitator is the person responsible for maintaining a balance between content and process, every participant shares in the responsibility. The Appendix contains a list of guidelines for participants that you might want to distribute and discuss at the next meeting you facilitate. It's an effective way to reach agreement on the role of participants and the responsibility they share for making your group meetings a success.

Problems that Arise in Meetings

As mentioned, members of a group will invariably differ in their perception of the situation, their purpose for being present, their past experience, and their personality. These four *P*s—perceptions, purpose, past, and personality—may disrupt the process and content.

A characteristic common to many meetings is that participants tend to become absorbed in the content and lose sight of their responsibility to help the leader in maintaining the process. They may have expertise or interest in the content, and their understanding of the process dimension (i.e., their ability to facilitate group interaction and synthesize the various input of members) may be relatively unsophisticated.

This places a heavy responsibility on the group leader to deal with a broad variety of people problems that can arise during a typical meeting. Four of the more common ones are described in the pages that follow, along with suggestions for dealing with them. Following these examples, you'll find some general guidelines for handling situations in which participants become problems in the eyes of the leader and other participants.

Participant is dominating

Situation
Participant is dominating, doing all the talking, answering the leader all the time, and monopolizing the group's time.

What Is The Problem?
If the participant has worthwhile experience to contribute and the others appreciate this and are benefiting from it, there may not be a problem at all (other than the threat they may be posing to the ego of the group leader).

However, if the other participants are beginning to show annoyance or are not thinking things through for themselves, you know that you have a problem. You want everyone to be free to participate and to share their input. If this is not happening, you should take action.

What Can Be Done?
There are a number of things you can do to correct the problem. They are listed in sequence according to severity. Try the simpler ones first, moving on to stronger measures if necessary. Here are the actions you might take:

- After a comment from the dominating participant, ask the rest of the group for their reaction; for example: "How do the rest of you feel about Pat's comment?" Their reaction will tell you and Pat whether there is a problem or not.
- Use other means of eliciting responses—ones that preclude Pat's dominating; for example: "I'd like you to discuss this question in three-person groups." And then assign the groups.
- Avoid eye contact with the dominating participant. When you pose a question, look at others for your responses. If Pat starts to answer with-

out being recognized by you, interrupt by rephrasing the question or by saying: "I'd like to hear from some others this time, Pat."
- Speak to the dominating participant during a break: "Pat, I'm real glad you're here, because I know I can always count on you to share your input. But I notice that others in the group are becoming dependent on you and not thinking things through for themselves. So I'm hoping you'll help me by giving the others a chance to share their input with us. Can I count on you?"

What Not To Do:
It's wise not to take on or attack the dominating participant. By doing so, you invite two likely outcomes: they may see it as a tug-of-war or test of strength and become even stronger and more dominating. Or they may retreat, avoid further contributions, and become sullen and negative. Because neither of these outcomes is desirable, it's better to try the previous suggestions.

Participants who never contribute

Situation
One or two people have not spoken or contributed during the past two meetings.

What Is The Problem?
All we know is that a couple of people aren't participating. We cannot assume from this that they are lost, bored, confused, disinterested, negative, or anything else. Certain people are reticent to speak up in groups. Therefore, the only problem we have is that we aren't getting any responses to let us know whether they are following the discussion.

What Can Be Done?
Our objective here is to get a reading on the silent ones and ease them into the group interaction without embarrassing them (because this could make them retreat even further).

The safest way to find out whether the silent ones are with you is to pose a question or give a brief assignment, then break the group into subgroups of 3 or 4 persons each to work on their response. As you circulate among the groups, pay particular attention to the silent ones, listening to their comments to see if there are any problems.

Let's say that your two silent people, Bill and Janet, each made good comments in their respective subgroups. After reconvening the full group, you might summarize by calling on several participants noting that you felt their comments should be shared with the full group, including Bill and

Janet. By reinforcing them for their comments, you have increased the likelihood that they will contribute to the full group in the future.

Another way to bring them into the group is to talk with them during a break to get their opinion on some things you're about to discuss. Then, when you've reconvened after the break, you can mention to the full group that: "I was talking about this issue with Bill during the break. In fact, Bill, why don't you share it with the group." The silent person now knows that their contribution is welcome, appropriate, and safe.

What Not To Do:
Because you don't want to embarrass silent participants into contributing, it's usually better not to call on them by name (unless you are inviting them to share an experience they are comfortable with, as with Bill or Janet).

Avoid putting any pressure on the silent one. It would not be appropriate, for example, to call on Janet by saying, "How about you on this one, Janet. We haven't heard from you yet." That wording implies to Janet that she hasn't been doing her fair share, and her answer better be good.

Participants who carry on side conversations

Situation:
Two or three people who sit together are talking softly among themselves and not paying attention to the leader. This has been going on for half a minute. The leader is becoming annoyed.

What Is The Problem?
It's not easy to know if we have a problem here. The leader is annoyed, but are the talking participants disturbing others? We don't know. Similarly, it would be dangerous to assume that the problem is that several participants are not paying attention. They might be sharing an insight on how to apply a new idea that they just picked up. It would be unfortunate if the leader were to embarrass them by asking them to rejoin the group, thereby interrupting their insight and punishing the very behavior that we're looking for.

What Can Be Done?
If the participants are seated around U-shaped tables or in a circle, the leader might walk slowly toward the talking participants, while looking at the rest of the group. In other words, the move should not be seen as an attempt to correct them. If their conversation is relevant to the meeting, they will feel no guilt in finishing their comments. However, if they are discussing last night's game on TV, they will probably rejoin the group as the leader approaches.

There are other actions that might be taken. The leader might pose a question to the group, then have participants discuss their answers in a two- or three-person group. Put them in groups to break up the clique that is talking.

Similarly, the leader might call on the participant who is sitting to the immediate left or right of the talkers. This is likely to get them to return to the group, because it would be rude and disruptive to continue their private conversation while the person next to them is trying to think and respond to the leader's question.

Of course, any participant who is being distracted by the private conversation can also take corrective action by saying to the leader (or whoever has the floor): "I'm sorry but I'm having trouble hearing you." This should lead the talkers to realize that they are annoying others. Or a more directive approach from a participant may be appropriate: "Excuse me, but I wonder if you two could rejoin the group. Some of us are having trouble hearing."

What Not To Do:
Although the leader is annoyed by the private conversation, it is important that he or she avoid resorting to parent-child ways of correcting the talkers. Examples of undesirable ways of taking corrective action:

- Scolding them with: "Are you two talking about something you'd care to share with the rest of us, or would you like to rejoin the group?"
- Calling on one of the talkers with a question. The likely reply is: "Would you repeat the question?" You must then bore (and punish) the others while you repeat the question and reward the talkers with extra attention.
- Lowering your voice or stopping your talking so as to catch the talkers, whose voices will stick out above the silence.

Participants who are antagonistic and negative

Situation:
Several participants are making their negative attitude known to others—by their side comments, scoffs, folded arms, and uncooperative or antagonistic attitude. This is creating an unhealthy climate and making things unpleasant for others.

What Is The Problem?
We don't know the problem. Perhaps the antagonists are attending against their will. Perhaps the topic isn't relevant. Perhaps they are negative about life in general and themselves in particular. Perhaps they feel negative toward the leader, or are bothered by the composition of the group.

Moreover, we don't know how widespread the negative attitude is. It's possible that the one or two antagonists are the tip of the iceberg, and that a number of others have similar negative feelings but are not as outspoken as the antagonists.

What Can Be Done?
To begin with, most leaders would like to know how widespread the negative attitude is (so they can know how much time to devote to dealing with it or whether there's any chance of changing it). The moment you get the first few negative comments from your antagonists, turn to the rest of the group and ask: "How do the rest of you feel about Harry's comment?" If they disagree or see Harry as a negative or disruptive influence, their response will tell you—and Harry—whether there's a problem.

Another way of disarming the antagonist is to put them to work—taking notes, serving as recorder at the flipchart, helping you to run an exercise. This serves to channel their thoughts and energy into productive activity.

If these methods don't work, it might be appropriate to take the antagonist aside during a break and talk to them: "Harry, I have the feeling that these sessions are not meeting your expectations, or aren't relevant to your needs. I wanted to discuss it with you since I certainly don't want to see you wasting your time here. Am I right?"

The dialogue that follows will lead to one of two outcomes: Harry either agrees to go along with the objectives and agenda without undermining it or he drops out of the group that he really wasn't part of to begin with. You gave him the option by dealing with him as a responsible adult.

What Not To Do:
It is wise not to take on the antagonist. First, you may lose. Second, a verbal fight may be just what the antagonist wants. Don't reinforce this undesirable behavior by granting them the stage. Third, many such arguments or debates do not have the possibility of a win-win outcome, so there is no way to get closure and satisfy everyone.

It is also wise not to insult the antagonists even if they are annoying others in the group. When you try to get them back in line in front of others, you are only adding to their negative feelings about the meeting and you. Moreover, you are resorting to parent-to-child techniques of discipline rather than dealing with the antagonist on an adult-to-adult basis. This may cause the climate of the meeting to deteriorate.

To Summarize
We have just examined four typical problems that are posed when participants fail to behave according to the norms of the group or the expectations of the facilitator. Although we discussed a number of specific actions that might be taken, several general guidelines can be deduced from our four examples. These guidelines can be applied to a wide variety of problems that arise whenever people meet to interact. Here they are:

- Separate symptoms from problems. Although we identified four examples of problematic behavior, in none of the cases did we know the root cause of the problem. The participant's undesirable actions have to be viewed as symptoms. And we are sometimes in danger when we try to treat symptoms without knowing what the problem is or even whether we have one (as in the case of the silent participant or the two participants whose side talk may have been highly relevant to the topic and their follow-up on it).
- Let the group handle the out-of-line participant whenever appropriate. When someone is dominating, being negative, being the joker, or picking on another group member, turn to the group and ask: "How do the rest of you feel about Harry's comment?" The feedback that you and Harry get will be much more useful and effective because it is coming from the group. This also enables you to maintain the neutral role so important for facilitators.
- Save face. Do not let a person lose face in the group. When someone is diminished in the eyes of other members of the group, their membership is in jeopardy. They may withdraw. In addition, other members will feel uneasy realizing that the same kind of thing might happen to them. A leader's responsibility is to maintain the integrity and unity of the group. This means facilitating the interactions in such a way that all members know the goals and are working together to achieve them.
- Maintain adult-to-adult relationships, not parent-to-child ones. Issues must be dealt with rationally, not emotionally, based on facts and opinions rather than on fictions, assumptions, and shaky or incomplete evidence. When the leader begins to play the parent role and treat respondents as children, they are likely to rebel and the problems will escalate. Theory X leaders are parent-to-child, expecting less from the group than they are capable of (and getting less). Theory Y leaders operate on an adult-to-adult basis, expecting more from the group than they thought themselves capable of (and getting more).
- Divide and conquer. Instead of dealing with the problem yourself, divide the group into subgroups of three to six persons. If unacceptable behavior arises, the members of the subgroup are likely to take care of it. In addition, the problem participant is more likely to feel a responsibility to contribute in acceptable ways in a small group, whereas in class they may want to show off or vent their hostility to an audience, hoping to gain support.

The more you can know about your participants in advance of the meeting, the better off you will be in dealing with their problems. Forewarned is forearmed. For example, if you know going in that Harry doesn't believe in the program but is coming to the meeting because his boss wants him there, you are much better prepared to address his negative feelings. Indeed, you might begin the meeting by noting that: "I know that some of you have reservations about the program we'll be discussing today. For example, Harry here feels that (you restate Harry's position), and I suspect others here have similar feelings. Have I stated your views accurately, Harry?"

You have just done two things to avoid having the meeting sink to a gripe session or venting of negative attitudes. First, you stole Harry's thunder and disarmed him. Second, you let the group know that there are two sides to the issues under discussion and that you aren't going to deal with only management's side.

A second way to prevent problems is to establish ground rules at the start of a meeting so that participants will know what is appropriate and inappropriate behavior and that it is the role of everyone present to make the meeting a success in achieving its goals. Anyone who doesn't buy in to the goals has the right to question them and seek clarification or defense of them. Thereafter, each participant should either accept them (and stay) or reject them (and leave).

A suggested set of ground rules, or guidelines for everyone (participants and facilitator alike), appears in the Appendix. By discussing these with your team, you should be able to take an ounce of prevention and avoid many problems of the types we've been discussing.

Self-Quiz on Meeting Leadership

1. In the space below each objective, indicate what you do or don't like about it.

    Our meeting this Thursday has three major objectives:

    - To look into the growing backlog of orders that haven't been filled.

    - To reduce our reject rate on the new machine.

    - To agree on the weekend work schedule for the next four weeks.

2. In the meetings you conduct, who fills each of the four roles previously discussed?

    Facilitator:

    Recorder:

    Group member:

    Manager or chairperson:

3. What can a facilitator do before holding a meeting to make its success more likely?

4. Describe the general procedure for dealing with a problem participant (i.e., your plan of what action to take).

5. One of your participants has challenged you or other members of the group on the last two suggestions just made. Another suggestion has just been made, and you see the challenger's hand go up. It's Harry again. He's waiting to be recognized. What should you do?

6. What are some of the key dos and don'ts that are good rules to follow in dealing with a problem participant?

7. In the space below, indicate with three or four examples what the ground rules and guidelines for participants might look like for the meetings you are likely to be conducting in the future.

9 Training And Development

- By the year 2000, more than 75% of the work force will need retraining to stay employed.
- The earth's storehouse of knowledge is doubling every 10 years.
- About 25% of today's jobs didn't exist 10 years ago.
- More than 90% of training is given on the job; under 10% in class by HRD staff.
- Only 15% of lifetime earnings are due to education; 85% are due to training.

Let's begin with a definition. Training is the process of imparting knowledge (K), attitudes (A), and skills (S) that the other persons must have to perform effectively. Learning (the other side of the coin) is the process of acquiring the K, A, and S needed to perform effectively.

Training is the process of closing the gap between the K, A, and S that an employee brings to the workplace (which trainers refer to as entering behavior) and the K, A, and S needed to perform the specific duties and responsibilities of the job (known as terminal behaviors). If we could hire employees with the desired terminal behaviors, training would be unnecessary. However, most organizations report that the gap between entering and terminal behaviors is widening every year. More training and more demanding training are required.

The demand exceeds the supply. Only a fraction of the demand can be filled by professional trainers—HRD staff, consultants, and schools. In an empowered organization, many employees are called upon to train, either one-on-one or in small groups. The instruction may be technical, dealing with operations (processes, equipment, or programs). At other times, the instruction deals with soft skills relating to teamwork, interpersonal relations, communications, and culture change (e.g., the paradigm shift from authoritarian and bureaucratic to empowered and democratic ways of getting things done).

In this chapter, we'll examine a number of concepts and skills you can apply when training others. Specifically, upon completing chapter 9, you should be able to:

- Define entering behavior and state why it should be determined.
- Indicate the two questions that a statement of terminal behavior should answer.
- Break the content of a training session down into K, A, and S.
- Plan a training session as a chain of S-R-F links.
- Ask questions that elicit relevant responses.
- Explain why S-R-F is a micro model and A-D-A a macro model.
- Illustrate the A-D-A model by applying it to your own instruction.

Every year organizations spend more and more time and money per employee on training and development. Less than 10 percent of this training is given by professional HRD specialists in formally scheduled classes. Most training is delivered in the workplace, at or near the job site, by experienced employees, supervisors, technical experts, team leaders, suppliers, or managers—in short, by facilitators.

Most of this more than 90 percent of on-the-job training is done one-on-one or in small groups, which is the focus of this chapter. We'll examine eight guidelines that will help you when you next facilitate a training session. But first let's see how effective you are in identifying some of the dos and don'ts of training.

In the script that follows, Connie is giving Jim an assignment that requires him to use an extension ladder to paint some windows that are up near the ceiling in a warehouse. Make notes in the margin to indicate what Connie did wrong or failed to do, referring to her comments by number.

Notes

1. Connie: You'll have to use the extension ladder to reach the upper ones. Do you know how it operates?

2. Jim: Yeah. I've got an aluminum one at home.

3. Connie: Good. Well set the ladder up so that it's leaning against the window sill at the top and out far enough at the bottom to make an angle of about 70° with the ground. Also, you want it extended far enough so that you can always grip the ladder with one hand while painting with the other. In other words, you should come back down the ladder and extend it farther up. Understand?

Notes

4. Jim: Yeah.

5. Connie: Okay. Let's make sure. Can you name the three things to remember when using an extension ladder?

6. Jim: Oh boy. Uhh ... let's see. Extend it far enough so that I can hold on to it while painting.

7. Connie: Good. That's one of 'em.

8. Jim: Keep the ladder slanted at a 70° angle.

9. Connie: Two down, only one to go.

10. Jim: And ... uhh ... are you sure there was a third?

11. Connie: Yes ... it's the first one I mentioned. Lean the top of the ladder against the window sill, not against the glass or the thin wood separating the panes.

12. Jim: Oh, yeah.

13. Connie: Okay. Now, once you get up there, what are you going to do? What will you paint first?

14. Jim: The thin wood strips that separate the panes.

15. Connie: Nope. You should start with the parts of the window that are farthest away from you—then work your way in toward you. It's a good rule to follow, whatever you're painting: first paint the part that is hardest to get to, most inaccessible or remote. Then end up with the parts that show the most. So if you are painting a chair or stool, you would first do the underside and the insides of the legs. The last things to paint are the fronts of the legs and the seat. Do you think you understand?

16. Jim: Yeah. I think so.

17. Connie: Good. Then go to it. You know where I'll be if you run into any problems. But I'll check back in a half hour or so to see how things are going.

18. Jim: Okay. I shouldn't have any trouble.

Connie's Weakness as a Trainer

Here are 12 failures we spotted—situations in which Connie was not being very effective in giving Jim instruction. Go back and check your own evaluation of Connie to see how many of these failures you were able to identify.

1. At the very start, Connie should have begun the instruction by explaining what Jim would be able to do when the instruction was over (the terminal behavior): "Jim, you'll be painting the windows today, so I'd like to take five minutes to make sure you know how to operate the extension ladder and how to paint the thin strips that separate the panes."
2. In line 3, Connie seemed to ignore Jim's response to the question: Do you know how it operates? Having one at home is not the same as knowing how it operates. Connie should have asked Jim to set up the ladder and demonstrate his understanding of how it operates.
3. In line 3, Connie gives out a lot of information without checking to see if Jim understands. There are three different pieces of information in this paragraph, three stimuli. She should have stopped after each one to get a relevant response from Jim and thereby make sure he understands.
4. Connie has no idea whether or not Jim can visualize a 70° angle. Is he carrying a protractor with him? It would have been better if she had asked Jim to show her what a safe angle would be by leaning the ladder against the wall. She could then find out if Jim understands what a safe angle really means.
5. Connie ends her lecture with "Understand?" This is a poor question. Jim is likely to answer yes whether or not he understands. In fact he may not even know whether or not he understands. In other words, the question does not elicit a relevant response, because trainees often can't tell whether or not they understand. Even if they don't understand, they may not want to say so to their instructor for fear of offending or of looking dumb.
6. In line 5, Connie asks Jim to name the three things. Naming them is not the same as doing them. Again, she is wasting time. Connie should have gotten Jim to do the three things and watched him while he did so. Many people are not verbal—especially those in jobs requiring physical skill over mental ability. Such employees are a lot more comfortable doing things than talking about them, especially when asked in a manner that is somewhat reminiscent of school days and classes in which the goal was to recite or repeat what the teacher had said.
7. In line 11, Connie should explain why she's giving these instructions. Or, it might be better if she had asked: "Jim, could you tell me why you'd lean the ladder against the wall above the window rather than against the lower sill?" His response would let her know if Jim understands ladder placement.
8. In line 13, this would usually be a good question. It is trainee-centered and shows that Connie wants to find out what Jim already knows before

teaching him. However, given her style of instruction up to this point, such a question probably looks like a test to Jim—a test of something he hasn't been taught yet. As such, it is likely to put Jim on the spot. He may be thinking: She must have covered this, but I don't remember it. In short, your style as instructor should be consistent. Switching from the information-centered style to a trainee-centered one may confuse the trainee.

9. In line 15, having just tried to find out what Jim already knows, Connie's "Nope" makes it look as if she had tried to set Jim up and to trap him. Instead, Connie should have led Jim on and helped him to see the adverse results of painting the thin wood strips first. People learn best, not by being told, but by experiencing the consequences of their actions. Connie should have asked why Jim feels it's best to paint the wood strips first.

10. In line 15, right after saying "Then end up with the parts that show the most," Connie should have thrown the ball to Jim, asking him: "Now Jim, let's see if you understand. Suppose you were going to paint a chair. How would you go about it? What parts would you paint first?" Any time you have to teach a rule or principle or procedure, it's a good idea to get the trainee to describe an example of it. This is one of the best ways to get feedback.

11. Connie ends her illustration of how to paint a chair or stool with: "Do you think you understand?" Again, this question is a poor one, because it is likely to get an irrelevant response. How does Jim know if he really understands until he does it? (This is the same problem we discussed in line 3.)

12. In line 17, Connie ends up with, "You know where I'll be if you run into any problems." That's poor. She should remain long enough to check Jim out and give him feedback. By so doing, she can correct poor techniques and reinforce good ones at the start.

The next two pages contain eight guidelines that Connie did not have the benefit of before she gave Jim instructions. You were also at a disadvantage, because you evaluated Connie without the benefit of these guidelines. After you've read them, you'll see why we spotted a dozen weaknesses.

Eight Learning Principles

1. Before giving instruction, find out what the person already knows about the topic or task you're about to teach. Find out what entering behavior they already have: the knowledge, attitudes, and skills that are relevant and prerequisite to the instruction you're about to give. This helps the trainee and the facilitator analyze the need for training.

Question: What did we just do at the start of this chapter to help you find out something about your entering behavior? What purpose does it serve?

2. Similarly, let the person know at the start of every training session the objectives, or terminal behavior that you expect following the training—what performance you're looking for in class and at work and why it is important.

   Question: Can you name at least three benefits of telling your trainees the terminal behavior you expect?

3. Your job is to close the gap between what employees bring to the training session and what they must leave with to perform effectively back on the job. Thus, training might be defined as the imparting of the knowledge, attitudes, and skills needed to close the performance gap between entering and terminal behavior. (If we could hire people with the desired terminal behavior, we wouldn't need training.)

   Question: What are some ways in which you can find out the entering behavior of the people you train?

4. Knowledge, attitudes, and skills are the three legs of the stool called behavior. People perform the way they do because of what they know, how they feel, and what abilities they possess. All three must be addressed during training; you can't have a one- or two-legged stool (see Figure 9.1).

   For example, consider how teenagers are taught to drive. Their performance depends on knowledge (how a car operates and the rules of the road). It also depends on attitude (safety and courtesy). And it depends on skill (balancing of accelerator and brake when standing on a hill waiting for the light to change).

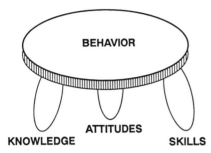
Figure 9.1

Question: Think of an operation or procedure that you're likely to teach someone in the group you serve as facilitator. Can you give an example or two of knowledge you will teach? Of attitude you want your trainee to develop? Of skills you will have your trainee practice?

5. People learn by responding to a variety of stimuli—the written and spoken word, models and illustrations, and real situation:

- The stimulus (S) is anything you show or tell the learner (visual, spoken, written).
- The response (R) is any action you get from the learner to show understanding.
- The feedback (F) is any information the learner gets to confirm understanding and reinforce the behavior.

    Question: Looking at the layout of these two pages, in what form is the stimulus that you're receiving? The response that you're making? The feedback that confirms your understanding?

6. Small S-R-F links make strong chains. The information you give your trainee (stimulus) should be bite size—not more than four minutes for each idea or policy or step in a procedure. Then you ask a question or make a request that gets the trainee to say something or do some-

thing (response), which usually takes about two minutes. Then you tell them how appropriate their response was (feedback), which averages no more than a minute. This is one link in your instructional chain.

Question: According to the time estimates noted above, how long is a typical S-R-F link in the instructional chain? How many links (ideas, key points, or rules) could you include in a 45-minute training session?

7. People learn best by making regular and active responses to the information you present, not by being a passive sponge, trying to absorb everything you tell them. But the responses must be relevant. That is, **they must** show that the trainee understands and can apply what you've just covered. Another meaning for S-R is Sale and Receipt. Your trainee's **response** must be a receipt that shows you that the sale (stimulus) took place.

Question: Instructors sometimes ask students: Do you understand? or **Do you have** any questions? Are such questions likely to get a relevant **response?** Why? What would be a better way of getting a receipt for the sale?

8. The S-R-F model is a micro model and requires about 7 minutes. But a typical training session lasts at least an hour or so and follows a macro model of acquisition-demonstration-application (A-D-A) as shown in Figure 9.2

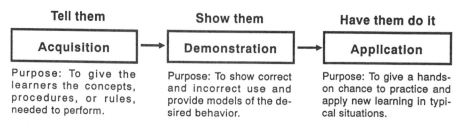

Figure 9.2

Question: How does the A-D-A model apply to courses you had in school? That is, what methods and media were used at each of the three stages of instruction?

The Desired Behavior

Let's assume that Connie has just gone through our critique and is now ready to do a much better job of teaching Jim how to place the ladder and paint the window. In the margin to the right of each of her comments, we've indicated the learning principle that she was applying in parentheses.

Connie:	Jim, you'll be painting the inside frames of the windows in the warehouse today, so I thought we ought to take a minute to make sure you know how to operate the ladder and how to plan your painting of the frames.	Set the objectives or terminal behavior. (2)
Jim:	Sounds good to me. I'm not sure if the 8-foot step ladder will reach.	
Connie:	You'll have to use the extension ladder on the upper ones, Jim. Do you know how it operates?	Find out the trainee's entering behavior.
Jim:	Yeah. I've got an aluminum one at home.	(1)
Connie:	Good. Well, let's use this one right here. Why don't you show me where you'd place it to paint that window up there? In other words, show me a safe angle for the ladder.	(1)
Jim:	Okay. (He sets ladder against window sill.) How's this?	
Connie:	Looks good. What will happen if you pull the base out farther away from the wall?	(1)
Jim:	The base might begin to slip and shoot out from under me.	
Connie:	And how about the opposite direction, what if you move the base closer to the wall?	(1, 6, and 7)

Jim:	Then the ladder will be too upright. If I lean back, it could go over backward.	
Connie:	Good. I notice that you have the ladder resting on the bottom window sill.	(7)
Jim:	Yeah. If I put it higher, it will be resting on the glass or thin framing between the panes. And they're not strong enough.	(6)
Connie:	True. But how are you going to reach the top of the window?	(6 and 7)
Jim:	I can stand on the top rung of the ladder.	
Connie:	That's a bit dangerous, isn't it? A safer way to reach the top is to extend the ladder farther up so that it rests on the wall above the window. Why is this safer, Jim?	(7)
Jim:	Uhh... because I can hold on to the ladder with one hand while I'm painting with the other.	
Connie:	Exactly. Now, once you get up there, what are you going to do? What will you paint first?	(1)
Jim:	The thin wood strips that separate the panes.	
Connie:	Why are you starting with these?	(7)
Jim:	Because they are the easiest to reach.	
Connie:	Yeah, but what's going to happen as you reach out to paint the sides of the window frame and the parts that are harder to reach? You may get your sleeve in the fresh paint.	(6)
Jim:	Okay, then I guess it would be better if I start by painting the parts that are farthest away—and work my way in.	
Connie:	Much better idea. In fact, that's a good rule to follow, whatever you're painting: first paint the parts that are the hardest to get to. Then end up with the parts that show the most. So if you're painting a chair or stool, what part would you do first?	(7)
Jim:	Uhh... the underside. And the inside of the legs.	
Connie:	What part would you save 'til last?	(7)
Jim:	The fronts of the legs and the seat.	
Connie:	Good. I can see that you understand. So, go to it. I'll be at my desk if you run into any problems. but I'll check back in a half hour or so to see how things are going.	
Jim:	Okay. I shouldn't have any trouble.	

Self-Quiz on Training and Development

1. What is meant by the term *entering behavior?* Why should you find this out before starting a training session?

2. What are the two questions you should answer in establishing the terminal behavior of a training session?

3. Let's assume you're going to teach someone how to drive a car. Give two examples of K, of A, and of S.

4. Apply the concept of chaining (S-R-F links in an instructional sequence) by describing how you might teach a new employee how to use a machine or a form that's used in the area in which you work. (Illustrate at least two S-R-F links, if you can.)

5. What's wrong with asking your learner questions like: Do you understand? or Do you have any questions?

6. Why is S-R-F called a micro model and A-D-A a macro model?

7. What are one or two examples of instructional methods used in each of the three stages of acquisition, demonstration, and application in the A-D-A model?

8. Drawing on a training program you're familiar with as an example, illustrate how the A-D-A model was applied.

10 Coaching And Counseling

In a survey of 300 top managers of General Electric, 90 percent felt that the most important factor contributing to their development was the coaching, counseling, and caring they received from another manager who took an interest in them and helped them develop. Only 10% gave credit to the training, rotation, or other personnel action that was taken in their behalf.

Everyone needs to have people to turn to when things are not going well. The frustration, stress, anxiety, uncertainty, and other pressures of life should be shared. The psychological word for it is catharsis—letting it out. Being a good listener is the biggest part of your role when someone seeks you out and asks for advice. What they usually want is empathy and a sounding board to help them talk things through.

That's your reactive role as coach and counselor, but you also have a proactive role. Someone's performance (output) or commitment (attitude) has deteriorated. You'd like to correct this and help them, but you don't want to pry. This is when you open the door with: "Pat, I've noticed that you don't seem to be yourself lately. I have the feeling that something is keeping you from giving your full commitment to the job. Is everything okay? Or has the highway of life thrown some bumps your way?"

If corrective counseling comes early enough, you can help Pat return to full productivity and job satisfaction. But if the situation has gone on undetected or ignored, the equation may not be reversible—permanent damage may have been done. People also need preventive maintenance.

In this chapter, you'll learn the major tools and techniques associated with your role as coach and counselor, whether you're filling the role reactively or proactively. Upon completing chapter 10, you should be able to:

- Identify at least five functions you fill when coaching and counseling.
- Describe the three steps of planning for a counseling session.
- Apply the 20 guidelines in your next coaching or counseling discussion.
- Give correction constructively, on an adult-to-adult basis.
- Translate negative feedback into positive, constructive statements.
- Review the 20 guidelines before counseling someone.
- Conduct effective, interactive, positive counseling sessions.

Throughout this book, you've seen numerous examples of the skills and values that go into being an effective facilitator: good listener, strong empathy, effective in using questions, ability to convert parent-to-child interactions into adult-to-adult relationships, and so on. Anyone who displays these qualities will be sought out by others who are looking for advice, for understanding, for a shoulder to cry on, or simply for attention.

We humans seek out other humans when we're faced with problems or decisions and want to discuss them. Your skills as a facilitator will make you especially helpful to others who want or need counseling.

I recall taking a college course on clinical psychology in which the professor read us a newspaper article about a woman in the midwest who advertised her services as follows: "I will listen to you for $3.00 per hour. Anything you care to discuss. I'm not a therapist, but I am a good listener. For an appointment, phone me at . . . ." The article went on to say that she was booked solid from 8:00 am into the evening, six days a week. (And $3.00 per hour in the 1950s would be worth three times more in today's market.)

The professor's point, and mine as well, is that people feel better after discussing something that is weighing on their mind. They usually don't expect solutions—or even expertise. Most people are happy with empathy and the opportunity to talk things through and hear themselves think.

When you are counseling someone, it's important to know what roles you're filling and what expectations the other person has of you. Here are some of the functions a facilitator fills during a counseling session. Check off the ones that might apply to you:

- A source of empathy (understanding) or sympathy (pity).
- An authority figure to add credibility or to sanction future actions.
- A sounding board to bounce ideas off or to think things through with.
- An advisor (but, if you're good, you'll avoid giving advice).
- A coach, mentor, champion, or other vested interest stakeholder.
- A neutral person who can be trusted with confidential information.
- A supervisor or team leader, responsible for performance standards.
- A friend, whom one feels better after sharing a burden with.

When you initiate a counseling session, you have time to plan your objective, your role, and your strategy. This is not the case when someone enters your office and launches the dialog with: "I've got a problem" or "I've got an opportunity I'd like to discuss and get your thoughts on it." Either way, your counseling should follow the following three-step process. And the 20 guidelines that follow will apply in most situations.

Planning Your Counseling Session

There are three steps to the planning of any interpersonal communication. First, we must assess the situation. Second, we must decide what our objectives of the interaction should be. Third, we must decide what information we have to give and to get, and in what sequence—that is, we must develop our game plan or strategy.

Most of us have objectives in mind (step 2) when we interact with others. What we tend to do, however, is spend too little time on steps 1 and 3. The following outline should be helpful.

1. Assess The Situation
What do I know about this other person? What information am I likely to need when we talk? Should I talk to anyone else before the session? Have I gotten all sides of the story? What are the other person's objectives likely to be? How are they likely to react to our talk?

2. Decide On Your Objectives
What are you trying to accomplish? Are you trying to solve the problem or attain the final objective, or does this session pave the way for another one? How will you know you've succeeded? What evidence will you look for to tell you that you can conclude the session? What specific action do you want each of you to take as a result of this session? What time frame is needed to carry out the desired action?

3. Develop Your Game Plan
What information do I want to give? What information do I have to get? What is my strategy for giving and getting information? What analogies, explanations, examples will I use to make my information understood? Where do I want to be directive and nondirective? Where is a high degree of bias appropriate? Where should I be neutral and avoid influencing the employee (i.e., low bias)? What are my opening and closing lines?

In a simple interaction that will last only 5 to 10 minutes, these three steps can be done mentally in a minute or so. But when the interaction is likely to take longer and be more involved (e.g., a performance appraisal, a problem-solving session, or a career discussion), it's a good idea to spend more time, perhaps 10 to 20 minutes, planning for the session.

In chapter 5, the self quiz asked you to evaluate Rudy's use of questions in correcting Ted. In our second example, Rudy had taken the time to go through these three steps by completing a coaching and counseling planning sheet. A copy is included on pages 175 through 178 of the Appendix. Take a moment to look it over. This planning sequence might help you to be better prepared the next time you need to conduct a counseling session. Our example illustrates a problem-solving counseling session, but the same process applies when you're counseling someone on a decision (e.g., early retirement, relocation, or going back to school).

Counseling: 20 Guidelines

Most of us have no trouble coaching people, teaching them how to do a job, or showing them ways of working more efficiently. But when it comes to counseling, we have a tendency to avoid it because we think it's not our business or to become an amateur psychologist and pry into their personal affairs or move from performance issues into personality traits.

Either extreme is wrong. To ignore a work-related problem is folly, and to invade their psyche can threaten the trust relationship that is so important to both of you. Here are some guidelines and observations to help you see your counseling role in perspective.

1. The first step in counseling someone is to reach agreement that a problem or opportunity exists and that your objective in discussing it is to find an appropriate way of responding to the situation.
2. Your role is not to solve employees' problems for them. Only they can do that. You can help them gain insight and develop a plan to correct the situation.
3. An employee with a disruptive problem is likely to feel uncertain, anxious, ashamed, or angry. If you cannot understand and be supportive of these feelings, you shouldn't counsel the person.
4. Your role is not to pass judgment or cause loss of face of the person you are counseling. Try to remain neutral, nonmoralistic, and shockproof. Employees need empathy and understanding, not sympathy and pep talks.
5. The more you listen, the more you will learn about the person you're counseling. This enables you to assess the situation better and achieve the desired objectives.
6. The more the employee talks, the more he or she is likely to take responsibility for personal behavior, know what to do in the future, and feel better for having talked it out.
7. The immediate problem is often a symptom of something bigger. Your role is to help the employee learn how to deal with future difficulties, not just the immediate problem.
8. All counseling sessions should be conducted in an atmosphere of confidentiality. The employee needs the assurance that your discussion will be kept private.

9. The focus of a counseling session should be on the employee's performance and not on personality. Your role is to help them to improve their performance but not change their personality.
10. Your counseling dialogue should be conducted on an adult-to-adult basis, not on a parent-to-child basis. Avoid blame or censure or advice; the employee must have authorship of the plan of action.
11. Make heavy use of nondirective questions that get the employee to open up and express feelings as well as facts. Use directive questions to confirm feelings.
12. Your comments during a counseling dialogue should seek out more information (searching) and show understanding and shared feeling (empathic) without being advising or critical.
13. Before any counseling session, answer these three questions: What is the situation here? What are my objectives? What strategy and questions will I use to achieve my objectives?
14. The climate should reflect mutual respect, acceptance of one another's view of the situation, and a desire to arrive at an outcome that you both find acceptable.
15. Counseling an employee with a performance problem is usually a high-stress situation for both of you. Don't put off the discussion; delay only adds to the stress. You'll both be relieved once you get the problem out in the open.
16. Approach counseling positively—you know that improvement will follow. When you express doubt (in words or negative signals) that the employee will improve, you risk a self-fulfilling prophecy and they will leave you with feelings of futility.
17. Build on strengths. Resist negative criticism: "This is the second time in four weeks that you've gotten your recap report in late." Instead, say: "One of the things I really like about your work is your ability to handle a heavy workload and meet deadlines. In fact, you might have too much on your plate if it kept you from getting your recap report in last Friday. What do you think?"
18. Avoid telling the employee what action to take. This puts the responsibility for a successful outcome on your shoulders. Instead, ask questions like: "What do you see as your options? How can the problem be avoided in the future? Which alternative do you think is most likely to work?" By using deductive questions, you get the employee's commitment to making a solution work.
19. Select a neutral setting for your discussion . . . a place that is private, nonthreatening, comfortable, and free of interruptions. It could be a corner in the employee lunchroom or cafeteria before or after the lunch hour.
20. End your counseling session by getting the employee to summarize: Maybe a good way to wrap up our discussion would be for you to summarize what we've agreed to and the time frame we have in mind. If the actions and consequences are serious enough, you might ask the

employee to summarize in writing the agreement reached. Or you might do so, asking them to either sign or make changes so that we know we understand one another.

Giving Correction Constructively

No matter how good your intentions and your careful wording of corrective feedback might be, the recipient is likely to be defensive and to regard your efforts as destructive. Although we face an uphill struggle whenever we need to give corrective feedback, there are guidelines for making constructive comments and helping others to accept them and act on them:

- Be descriptive rather than evaluative. Describe your reaction to it without being judgmental. Give the party freedom to accept or reject your reaction.
- Be specific. Don't generalize from a sample of one or two instances. For example, instead of saying: "You dominate and intimidate others," you might say: "At the meeting I felt you came on pretty strong when you. . . . "
- Address the needs of the person you're correcting. Maintain their self-esteem and personal worth. Relate the desired behavior to an increased level of self-esteem.
- Address specific behavior that the other person can do something about. Do not address personality issues. Instead of saying: "Your ego got in the way," you might say: "You used a lot of references to your boat and expensive car that might have kept the committee from listening to your proposal objectively."
- Get the other person to ask for feedback. Give only a little. Then stop and ask if they want you to elaborate and share your other perceptions. Make the session a dialogue by involving the other person.
- Select the best time to give the feedback in a private (confidential), unhurried, relaxed manner. Ask if this is a good time. If the other person's priorities are elsewhere, agree on another time and place.
- Have the other person summarize your concerns and the action to be taken. This will let you know if the message was understood and accepted. It may also reinforce their resolve to take corrective action.
- Be sure you have a sufficient sample of behavior and aren't jumping to erroneous conclusions based on an isolated instance. Check with others to see if the behavior that bothers you is bothersome to others.

The next page shows three examples of negative feedback and how it might have been converted into a more acceptable and effective form.

Constructive Feedback: Some Examples

Example of Negative Feedback	What's Wrong	Reworded—Positive and Constructive
You never clean up your work area or put things away. It looks messy to visitors, and it means that you can't work as efficiently when you have to spend a lot of time trying to find things that got buried. Sloppy work habits can be a reflection of sloppy thinking.	Generalizations: You never, and You can't. Irrelevant and unfair: A reflection of sloppy thinking.	We had visitors come through yesterday. I wanted to bring them by to meet you but decided not to, since your work area was rather messy. Any chance of your putting it in order during the next day or so?
Your presentations are good but they lack sparkle and color. The facts are all there and your flow of ideas is good, but I'm afraid that people tune you out because they lose interest in your monotone and the somewhat dull way in which you present the message. Try to add a little zing to your presentations, and you'll find that people will really sit up and take notice.	Judgmental: They lose interest in your monotone and the somewhat dull way in which	I really like the content of your presentation—the facts, the flow of ideas—you've done your homework. Which means we're ready to take the next step: presenting the message. I've got some ideas—you probably do, too—on how we can add zing to your presentations.
I know you're anxious to be promoted to branch manager, but you've got a ways to go in developing your people-handling skills before you're ready to handle a job like that. On the task-handling side, you're great—good accuracy, always on time, and your reports are well organized and well written. But you must learn to develop some patience and tact and listening skill with people before you're ready for branch management.	Very negative: You've got a ways to go ... and You must learn to develop... . On tasks, the feedback is behavioral and specific: On time, well written. But on people, it's too general: Develop patience and tact.	There are two sides to branch management: handling people and handling tasks. Which of these do you think you're best at? ... Why? ... What actions can we take to bring your interpersonal skills up to the same levels? ... How can I help?

Self-Quiz on Coaching and Counseling

1. On a separate sheet of paper, rewrite these three negatives to make them constructive and positive:
    - You're always rushing to get things done. This means that you don't take the time to do it right, and other people end up trying

to correct the mistakes you made. That wouldn't have to be if you'd only take the time to plan how you're going to do a job, then do it right the first time.

- You have an annoying habit of not listening to people. You don't look at them; you seem preoccupied with your own thoughts. When you're at your desk, you read things and shuffle papers when others are talking to you. As a result, you miss a lot of facts and feelings, and go off with misconceptions and incomplete information. I hope you can do something about it.

- Several times during recent months you've talked with other department heads to get things from them or their people. This is in violation of the chain of command principle. Talk to me first. If I feel that another department head should be contacted, I'll talk with them or arrange for you to do so. In other words, let's not have any more direct contact with senior managers without coming to me first.

2. What are the three steps of planning for a counseling session? What do you need to know (questions to be answered) in each step?

3. You examined a list of 20 guidelines. Can you recall seven or eight of them now? What use, if any, do you see for this list?

4. What are some of the things you can do to ensure that corrective feedback is positive and constructive? (Can you recall at least four of the eight?)

5. Compare your rewrites of question 1 (above) with these examples:

    - One of the things I really like about your work is that you get a lot of things done. You don't waste time. In fact, you seem to be rushed at times. Do you feel rushed or that you have too much work? ... The reason I ask is that sometimes you make careless errors on things I'm sure you know how to do. I don't know if it's the work load or your zeal. What do you think?

- Sometimes when we're talking at your desk, you seem distracted. Maybe I shouldn't start to talk when you've got projects on your desk that are on your mind. Or maybe we should meet in my office or somewhere else where I won't feel shut out of your thoughts. Got any ideas?
- It's natural that when I'm out of town or away from my desk and you need things from other department heads or their people, you've gone to them. And now some of them are wondering why I didn't make the request—or even why I couldn't give you what you needed without bothering them. So, whenever you can, talk to me first. Okay?

11 Analyzing And Solving Problems

Four hard-to-learn lessons about problem solving:

- Many problems aren't your problems. Leave them alone. It's only your problem if it's keeping you from achieving your objectives.
- Many times we treat symptoms and never get to the root causes. No wonder the same or other symptoms recur: we never identified the problem (or its cause) or dealt with it.
- A "quick fix, immediate" results society creates and multiplies problems. Today's emphasis on TQM, benchmarking, and continuous improvement (*Kaizen*) is an attempt to reverse the trend and reduce problems.
- Once the real problems are identified and solved, precautionary measures or maintenance systems must be put in place to prevent recurrence.

Many courses exist on problem solving—the 1993 ASTD Buyer's Guide & Consultant Directory lists 78 sources. Empowered organizations typically have training programs in place to teach the concepts and skills of problem analysis and solution. This chapter won't reinvent the wheel. It does provide three job aids and permission to use them as guides for use with your work groups. Each is a flowchart, and they appear on pages 145–147.

Upon completing this chapter, you should be able to:

- Give at least three reasons people may avoid solving a known problem.
- Distinguish between problem and symptom, illustrating with an example.
- Describe the process for locating a problem not caused by human action.

- State what must be done after solving a problem to prevent recurrence.
- Apply a six-step process to a current or recent work-related problem.

Most of the problems we're called upon to solve could have been avoided. That is, action could have been taken to reduce or eliminate the causal factors. Why, then, don't people take the necessary steps? Here are a few of the typical excuses:

- We were too busy. I knew that the situation was precarious but didn't have time to take care of it.
- Let's not worry about problems that aren't bugging us right now. No need to fix the leaky roof on a sunny day!
- Nobody told me to take care of that. It's not my job anyway.
- I've told them to take care of that. If we have a real problem, it will serve them right—maybe even teach them a lesson.
- Around here, it's productivity that counts. Nobody wins hero buttons by looking for potential problems that may never occur.

All of these reasons are typical responses of people who are not empowered—people who put blinders on instead of helping others to remove blinders (which, of course, is what facilitators do). Even when employees are motivated to tackle a problem, they're often off to a bad start. We asked a number of companies to state a key problem that they wanted to correct. The answers looked something like this:

- Our employees are using sick days for personal business.
- Our supervisors are not conducting meaningful performance appraisals.
- Our machinists are not following the prescribed safety procedures.
- Our salespeople are not selling our full product line.

In each of these responses, a symptom has been identified. But there is no indication of the root cause, or problem. We must learn to ask why. And if the answer is partial, to ask why again—until the likely causes have been identified. These four statements describe symptoms, not problems.

The reason many problem-solving courses fail to have a significant impact on the performance of participants is that they address symptoms and impart simplistic formulas for workplace behavior without getting to the root problems that are keeping such behavior from occurring in the workplace.

The following pages contain flowcharts that are useful in diagnosing problems (i.e., the root causes of a performance deficiency). The deficiency might be in the equipment (system or procedure), as shown in the first chart. Or it might be in the person responsible for performance, as shown in the second chart. The third flow chart outlines a six-step process for tracking a problem, from its initial definition to its solution.

Analyzing And Solving Problems

Procedure for Analyzing a Performance Deficiency: Focus on the Equipment Portion of the Equation

Situation: Equipment isn't doing what we want it to do.

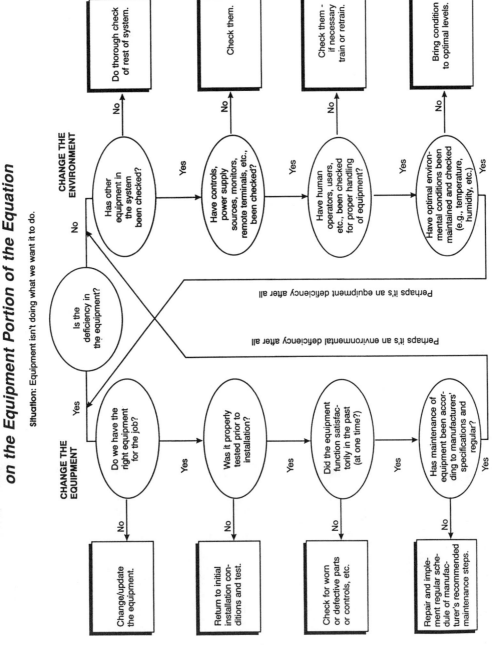

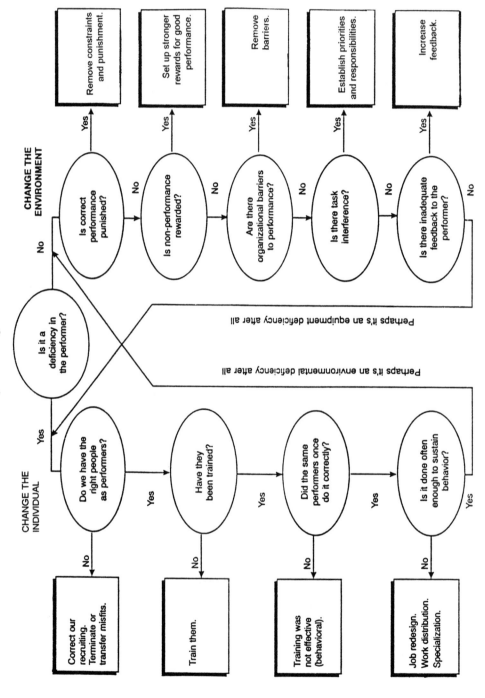

Analyzing And Solving Problems

The Problem-Solving Process: An Overview

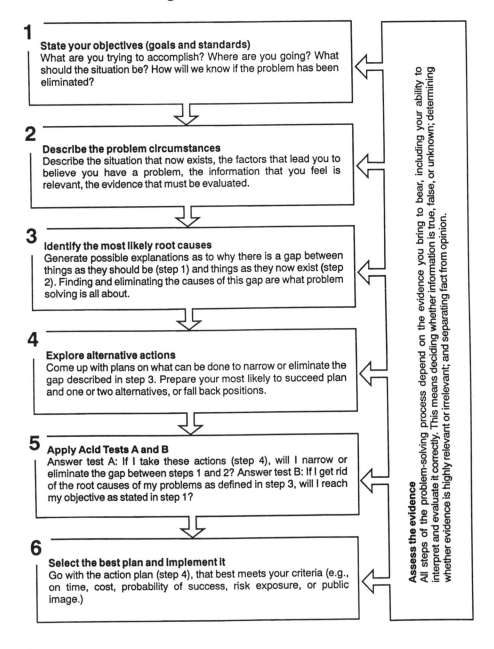

1. State your objectives (goals and standards)
What are you trying to accomplish? Where are you going? What should the situation be? How will we know if the problem has been eliminated?

2. Describe the problem circumstances
Describe the situation that now exists, the factors that lead you to believe you have a problem, the information that you feel is relevant, the evidence that must be evaluated.

3. Identify the most likely root causes
Generate possible explanations as to why there is a gap between things as they should be (step 1) and things as they now exist (step 2). Finding and eliminating the causes of this gap are what problem solving is all about.

4. Explore alternative actions
Come up with plans on what can be done to narrow or eliminate the gap described in step 3. Prepare your most likely to succeed plan and one or two alternatives, or fall back positions.

5. Apply Acid Tests A and B
Answer test A: If I take these actions (step 4), will I narrow or eliminate the gap between steps 1 and 2? Answer test B: If I get rid of the root causes of my problems as defined in step 3, will I reach my objective as stated in step 1?

6. Select the best plan and implement it
Go with the action plan (step 4), that best meets your criteria (e.g., on time, cost, probability of success, risk exposure, or public image.)

Assess the evidence
All steps of the problem-solving process depend on the evidence you bring to bear, including your ability to interpret and evaluate it correctly. This means deciding whether information is true, false, or unknown; determining whether evidence is highly relevant or irrelevant; and separating fact from opinion.

Self-Quiz on Problem Solving

1. What are some of the reasons people may avoid solving a problem, even when they know the root causes and have the needed skill and resources?

2. Using a recent problem you've faced as your example, illustrate the difference between a symptom and a problem.

3. Verify your understanding of the process for locating a technical (not caused by human error) problem by describing the troubleshooting sequence you would follow. Then compare your description with the flow chart on page 145.

4. Follow the same assignment noted in question 3, but do it for a problem caused by a human error or deficiency. Then compare your description with the flow chart on page 146.

5. After a problem is solved, what must be done to prevent its recurrence?

6. Select a current or recent problem you faced at work and describe the action that was or was not taken at each of the six steps of the problem-solving process as outlined on page 147.

12
Making Decisions

Decision making is one of the more difficult responsibilities to delegate or get work groups to do. Managers have trouble letting go, and employees fear the consequences of a bad decision. Both parties feel more comfortable when they can push the decisions upstairs. An understanding of the decision-making process can go far in getting people to accept responsibility and to make effective decisions.

When we were children, our parents made many decisions for us. They selected our clothes, diet, friends, hobbies, and leisure time activities. But as we matured, we gradually took on the responsibility for making these decisions ourselves. Most of us had no problem—we understood the choices our parents had made for us and we were strongly influenced by the values they had imparted.

A parallel situation occurs when organizations attempt to empower their employees. As work groups mature and as the number of managers available diminishes, employees are called on to make decisions that were once made by managers. They will succeed to the degree to which the three conditions just noted are present:

- The weaning must be gradual, proceeding from simpler and safer decisions to more complex and challenging ones.
- Different choices, options, or alternatives must be available, and employees must know or learn what they are.
- The values of the organization must be shared, so that decisions are made within these parameters (i.e., guidelines, policy, and culture.)

This last condition can pose a problem because traditional values and culture discouraged employees from making decisions: Too risky . . . That's your supervisor's job... Management is more experienced. Today the paradigm shift that accompanies empowerment tells us that employees must make decisions, individually and as team members. But are they ready, willing, and able?

It's our role as facilitators to see that these three conditions are met, and that the decision-making process outlined in this chapter is understood and applied. Upon completing chapter 12, you will be able to:

- Identify differences and similarities between problem solving and decision making.
- State the factors that determine whether groups or individuals should make a decision.
- Describe the 10-step decision-making process, illustrating it with examples.
- Indicate the two factors that receive numerical ratings, with reasons for each.
- Distinguish between limits, desirables, risks, and options by defining each.
- Construct a decision matrix to help in reaching a complex decision.
- Construct a 2-by-2 table to help in reaching a simple (binary) decision.
- Coach others in how to use the tools taught in the chapter.
- Facilitate the transition into empowered decision making.

Every day we make hundreds of decisions. Some are almost automatic, such as deciding to close the door after you. Some involve no risk at all, such as the decision of whether to wear your tweed overcoat or your leather one. Some have a modest risk, such as whether to get off the expressway and find a gas station (thereby possibly missing your flight) or to stay on the expressway (thereby possibly running out of gas before reaching the airport). Some involve larger stakes, such as purchasing a home or deciding whether to buy another car or to replace the transmission in your current one. These are personal decisions.

At work our day is filled with decisions that affect our ability to manage and to reach organizational objectives. Most of these decisions can be made in a matter of seconds. Typical examples include things like this:

- Should we write Tom a warning memo, talk to him about it, or overlook it?
- How can I best show Jean my appreciation for working over the weekend?
- What will we send to Mildred who just entered the hospital?
- Who should attend the summary report meeting?
- Should we have our duplicating department run it off or give it to an outside printer?
- When do I want the new equipment to be delivered?
- Should we have an office party for Sharon's engagement to Bill?

These kinds of decisions usually do not require much deliberation. The options are relatively limited, the criteria and limits are fairly well understood, there's often a lot of precedent, and the consequences of a wrong decision are not earthshattering. The vast majority of decisions we make are of this type. Peter Drucker makes the distinction between tactical decisions and strategic decisions. These examples are tactical and do not require very rigorous analysis. Nor do they plague us with doubts, anxiety, and second thoughts.

Our concern, however, is with the difficult decisions you make—the ones that require research, analysis of alternatives, concern with risk, and your desire to make the process more objective (data-based, quantitative, or scientific) and less subjective (intuitive, or biased) Here are some typical examples of the kinds of decisions that are a bit more difficult:

- Should we have our own computer people do the programming, or have it done outside?
- Is it better to buy or lease a word processor during the first year of operation?
- Should I combine Joe's area with Tom's, or hire another person to replace Joe?
- Which of the four bids should I select?
- Will an executive recruiter or an ad in the *Wall Street Journal* do better?
- Should we reorganize the assembly area into self-directed teams?
- Does flextime (flexible working hours) make sense for my work group?

These decisions require a lot of input information to be weighed, the consequences are complex, and thousands of dollars are at stake. These are the kinds of decisions this chapter can help you make with much greater comfort and precision. Of course, nothing can guarantee that your decisions will be correct, because nobody can control the future events affecting them. But we can evaluate and assign weights to every factor that goes into a decision, thereby increasing the probability that your decisions will produce the results you want.

Before we get into the 10-step decision-making process, let's distinguish between problem solving and decision making. Problem solving is the process of correcting a situation that is keeping us from achieving something we want (e.g., a goal or objective, a norm or standard of desired performance). The focus is on finding the cause of deviation or blockage and then taking corrective action that will restore the situation to normal. Problem solvers speak largely in the past tense—something has happened to keep us from getting what we want.

In contrast, decision making is the process of assembling and evaluating information relating to each of several alternatives so as to select the one most likely to achieve our objective. The focus is on taking action in new and often unfamiliar areas. Often we're dealing with a situation that may never have existed before. Decision makers therefore speak largely in the future tense.

Having distinguished between the two, we can now identify a number of similarities. Both processes must begin with a description of the situation and a definition of the objectives (i.e., standards, goals, or conditions) that must be met. Both of them involve the identification of alternatives. And both require a high degree of analytical skill and patience as well as an awareness of one's own values and personal biases.

Moreover, once a root problem has been identified, there may be more than one course of action available for reducing or eliminating it. This means decision making. What are the probable effects of each? The risks associated with each? In short, if we distinguish between problem analysis and problem solving as many experts do, decision making must be seen as an integral part of problem solving.

Similarly, if we are engaged in making a major decision (such as buying a house or hiring an assistant) we may encounter problems that keep us from making a good decision (e.g., the price is outside our reach or there are no acceptable alternatives). We must then interrupt our decision-making sequence to engage in a little problem solving that will remove the barriers and give us enough options to continue on our decision-making way.

Following is a series of statements; some describe a problem to be solved, and others describe a decision to be made. Place the initials PS or DM in front of each to indicate whether the focus is on problem solving or decision making. After you've completed the eight items, compare your responses with the ones printed in the footnote on page 156.

_____ A group of supervisors is trying to find out why the new equipment is not running at the levels of efficiency advertised by the manufacturer.

_____ An employee and his wife are discussing whether or not he should take the early retirement package his company has offered him.

_____ A recent college graduate who has been given job offers by three different companies must let them know whether she accepts or not.

_____ The department head has decided that it's time to find out why people are coming back from lunch after 75 to 90 minutes rather than after the hour that is allowed.

_____ A manager must tell his boss whether or not he wants the promotion that involves relocating to another state.

_____ A quality circle of employees is trying to identify the cause for the increased number of rejects in last week's production run.

_____ A woman is checking the roll of paper in the fax machine to see why copies are coming out with overlapping lines of type.

_____ A family of four is wondering whether to go to the shore or the mountains for their vacation and whether the teenage son should be allowed to stay home.

Answers follow on page 156.

Who Makes the Decision?

In the traditional bureaucratic organization, decisions are made by managers and carried out by employees. Empowerment has moved the responsibility for decisions into the ranks of employees. However, certain kinds of decisions must be made by management and other kinds are best handled by the employees who must implement them and live by the consequences of them.

Figure 12.1 describes four types of decisions as determined by two variables: The need for quality that calls for expertise, and the need for commitment that calls for participation. The question of who is in the best position to make a decision can be answered by determining the relative strength of the two needs, quality and commitment.

	TEAM DECISIONS	JOINT DECISIONS
	High commitment, low quality	**High commitment, high quality**
NEED FOR COMMITMENT (High → Low)	Some decisions are more important to the workgroup than to the manager; for example: Who gets which parking spaces or new tools, vacation schedules, the cafeteria menu. If management does not have a stake in the outcomes, then the group alone should decide. They will be more satisfied with the outcome.	Some management decisions affect what, when, and how the team does their work; for example: Identifying and dealing with policies that are outdated or interfering with productivity. Here the manager works with the team members, and the outcome must be acceptable to all.
	ROUTINE DECISIONS	**TECHNICAL DECISIONS**
	Low commitment, low quality	**Low commitment, high quality**
	Neither the issue nor the outcome require much deliberation; for example: Which supplier to buy pencils or paper clips from. Here the manager alone decides (or delegates the decision). No need to bother anyone else.	Sometimes correctness of the decision is the single most important factor; for example: Selecting the right computer system, deciding how to go public, determining where to drill for oil. Manager decides on basis of strong technical advice.

Low ——————→ NEED FOR QUALITY ——————→ High

Figure 12.1

From Managing to Empowering

This chart outlines a 10-step process for making a major decision. Notice that the order of steps 3 to 4 and steps 8 to 9 can be reversed depending on the nature of the decision. On the following page, you'll find an illustration of these 10 steps with a decision that is familiar: buying a car.

The Process of Decision Making

1. Define the situation that led to the need for a decision.
What factors make a decision desirable now?

2. State the purpose and the objectives to be met.
What are we trying to accomplish? How will we know we've succeeded?

3. Specify the criteria: Limits and desirables.
What factors are my upper and lower limits? What factors are most important to me?

4. Generate alternative courses of action.
What are my options? Have I considered all feasible alternatives?

5. Establish rankings to reflect relative importance of desirables.
How important is each "desirable" to me? How can I quantify this?

6. Quantify the factors associated with each alternative.
What data do I have on each option? How does each score?

7. Multiply ranking values (criteria) by scores (of each alternative) to get weighted totals.

8. Assess the risk.
What could go wrong with each alternative? With what probability? With what seriousness?

9. Select the best decision
Which alternative got the best overall score?

10. Implement decision and monitor results.
How can I increase the chances of success for the alternative I selected?

Answers to quiz on page 154 (from top to bottom): PS, DM, DM, PS, DM, PS, PS, DM.

Illustration: Buying a Car

1. Carol and Bill need a car. They've been driving a six-year-old model that is in the repair shop every month or so. It's costing them more to keep it running than it's worth.
2. They want a dependable second vehicle so that they can each have transportation. They already own a new compact.
3. Bill buys a lot of lumber and sheetrock for home improvement projects. It would be desirable to be able to carry it home inside the vehicle rather than on the roof rack. Also, they've decided not to spend more than $6,000 and not to buy anything older than four or five years, which probably means not less than $3,000.
4. They might buy or lease. They might get a station wagon, a van, a pick-up truck with cap, a minibus. They might trade in the six-year-old model at a used car lot or buy from the classified ads in the newspaper.
5. Because Carol and Bill have two kids, they decide that a station wagon or van gives the flexibility of hauling lumber or the family in comfort. Limits: Seating for five and space for 4-×-8-foot sheets of lumber or sheetrock. Desirables: Fuel efficient (8), rear door hinged to open upward rather than sideways or down (10), price as low as possible (5), low mileage (4), color and styling (2). All ratings are on a 10-point scale.
6. They narrow the selections down to a Buick, Plymouth, Ford, and Mercury. Then they make up a 4-column comparison: different wagon in each column with the features assigned scores. For example, on fuel efficiency, they learn that the four wagons they're considering get the following figures on miles per gallon: 12, 16, 18, and 8, which they divide by two (lowest common denominator) to get scores of 6, 8, 9, and 4 respectively.
7. Now they can multiply their step 6 scores by their step 5 rankings to get the weighted totals. Continuing with our fuel efficiency example, in step 5 that was considered to be a fairly important desirable, with a rating of 8. So Carol and Bill multiply their four fuel efficiency scores (6, 8, 9, 4) by 8 to get 48, 64, 72, and 32, which they enter across their four-column comparison. They do the same for every other desirable.
8. Mechanic gives the wagon a test drive and checks out all systems to see that the vehicle is sound, that it passed the last inspection, and that the new spray paint job under the hood isn't hiding any defects.
9. Carol and Bill now select the wagon that obtained the highest rating in step 7 and that gets the mechanic's approval in step 8, (If their first choice fails to get the mechanic's approval, they then move to their second choice, and have the mechanic check it out.)
10. Carol and Bill set up a preventive maintenance program to change the oil and rotate the tires every few thousand miles to get the best return on their decision.

Desirable Quality	relative importance	Buick		Plymouth		Ford		Mercury	
fuel efficient	8	48	6	64	8	72	9	32	4
rear door	10	70	7	40	4	100	10	100	10
price	5	50	10	15	3	35	7	20	4
mileage	4	28	7	40	10	16	4	40	10
color and styling	2	16	8	6	3	10	5	14	7
well taken care of	7	35	5	42	6	21	3	56	8
Totals		247	43	207	34	254	38	262	43

Figure 12.2

The decision matrix shown in figure 12.2 was prepared by Carol and Bill. It follows the steps referred to on the prior two pages. Look back as you need to.

- They set four limits that determined what station wagons they would and wouldn't consider: must not cost more than $6,000, must not be older than 5 years, must have seats for five, and must have 4'-×-8' hauling space after removing rear seat).
- They then listed the desirable qualities down the left side, and assigned a number to each, using a scale of 1 to 10, to reflect its relative importance (because not all desirables are equally important).
- Next they selected four station wagons that met their limits, and added a column for each. (Although there is no limitation to the number of options, or columns, that can be added to a matrix, for practical reasons the number rarely exceeds six and is usually around three or four.)
- By dividing each square into two areas, Carol and Bill made space for their two numbers. The lower space shows the relative rating they gave to each of the four wagons (working horizontally across rows and using a scale of 1 to 10). And the upper triangle contains the number they

got by multiplying this relative rating of the vehicle by the relative importance of this desirable quality.
- Once the matrix was completed by working horizontally across the four columns, Carol and Bill were ready to work on each column vertically by adding up the six scores in the triangles. This gave them the totals shown in triangles at the bottom of each column.
- As can be seen, the Mercury is clearly the first choice of Carol and Bill, with a total score of 262. If it's no longer available, they should move to their second choice, the Ford.

Some Observations on Assigning Weights

1. You might wonder if it was necessary to assign weights to the relative importance of each desirable quality. Why not simply rate each vehicle on each desirable and avoid all the triangles and multiplication?

    If all of the desirable qualities are equally important (or nearly so), there is no need to add the triangles. However, they do provide a more accurate reflection of the value you place on each desirable. For example, on Carol and Bill's matrix, the Ford came in as second choice (at 254). If they had not used triangles and simply added the six scores in each column without factoring them, the Buick (43) and the Mercury (43) would be tied for first choice. However, by assigning weights to reflect the relative importance of each desirable, they got a more accurate measure of their preferences, and we see that the Buick is really Carol and Bill's third choice at 247.

2. Carol and Bill used a 10-point scale to rank the desirables and again to rank each car. (Actually, no car got a rating lower than 3, so their 10-point scale really turned out to be an eight-point scale—from 3 to 10.)

    But why a 10-point scale? Why not a six-point scale? Or any other number of ordinals? The number you select should be determined by the number of discriminations or degrees of difference you feel you can make. And 10 is probably on the high side—you might be more comfortable assigning ratings on a five-point scale.

3. Sometimes a decision matrix will list a desirable quality that can only occur in one of several ways. For example, if automatic transmission is preferred to a stick shift, these are the only two options. In such cases, you have to select two ratings to reflect the relative difference in importance.

Looking at the rear door entry on Carol and Bill's decision matrix, we see only three numbers used to rate the four cars: 4, 7, 10. This is because there are only three rear door options available on a station wagon: the door can only open up, down, or sideways.

Why didn't Carol and Bill use 8, 9, and 10 to rate the three different door options? Because ratings this close would indicate that it really didn't matter much as to how the door opens. But we know from the rating of 10 assigned to this desirable quality that it's the most important one on the list. Hence their decision to use 4, 7, and 10. (They could also have selected 2, 6, and 10—or any other three numbers reflecting their preference for each of the ways a rear door opens.)

When Decisions Are Binary

Many decisions are binary—select A or B, act now or later, repair or replace. A simple 2-by-2 table will serve in such situations. In Figure 12.3, you'll see an example. Here's the situation. The manager of administrative services is faced with a decision. Seems that Jim, supervisor of the printing shop, has a mounting backlog of jobs to be printed. He lacks a system for prioritizing and assigning delivery dates as he gets jobs. Shirley, whose word processing section generates most of the camera-ready copy that Jim prints, is very good at scheduling and organizing her work.

The manager of administrative services must now decide whether he should work with Jim to find out what the problem is and help him overcome it or whether Shirley and Jim should work together so that she can handle the scheduling of jobs from start (typesetting) to finish (printing). As you can see from the weights assigned in each box, the second option is the better one. The following description of the situation was prepared by the manager of administrative services to help in making the decision.

The Situation

- Managers are telling me about Jim's late deliveries of printing.
- Jim reported at staff meeting that backlog is building up.
- Some departments are taking their jobs to outside printers.

The problem: Is Jim understaffed? I thought so until my talk with Shirley today. She thinks that Jim lacks a system for scheduling and prioritizing, and the guts to stick to it and not be talked into making every job a crash project.

I have two options:

1. work with Jim and help him set up a scheduling system to organize and prioritize his work.
2. let Shirley handle scheduling for Jim's work as well as her own.

Options	Advantages	Disadvantages
1. Work with Jim	Scheduling is part of his job. It's Jim's responsibility. (3)	He doesn't like it or want to do scheduling. He also can't say no. I don't have the time or skill to coach him. Shirley would have to and he'd balk at that. (7)
2. Let Shirley do scheduling	She's willing to, if Jim will accept it. She's being blamed for his late stuff now. Some 80% to 90% of his work comes from Shirley's group, so she's scheduling it already. By having Jim work with her, he can learn her skills in a nonthreatening setting (8)	Possibility that Jim may feel stripped of part of this job, or that Shirley will feel burdened with his work. But this is unlikely. (3)

Figure 12.3

Self-Quiz on Decision Making

1. As you matured and moved from childhood into adulthood, three conditions were necessary for you to make decisions that were formerly handled for you by your parents. These same conditions apply to organizations as they empower their employees. What are the three conditions?

2. What are the major differences and similarities between problem solving and decision making?

3. On a separate piece of paper draw a 2-by-2 table to illustrate the two factors that determine who should make a decision. Follow the format of figure 12.1, then complete the table by giving an example of a decision in your workplace for each of the four boxes on the table.

4. On a separate piece of paper construct a decision matrix for a typical decision you might face at work or at home (e.g., which candidate to hire or promote, which copy machine or fax to buy, which home or apartment to select). List at least five desirable qualities and three options on your matrix. Then indicate what rating scale (how many numbers) you would use to rank your desirables and your options. (Don't bother doing the ratings or the multiplication unless the example you picked is a real one and you're ready to reach a decision.)

5. A decision matrix includes a list of your desirables and your options. What are the other two factors (steps) that are not shown on the matrix? Why aren't they shown?

6. A manager has asked for your advice about whether she should organize her department of 14 people into two self-directed teams or get an assistant manager (because she is stretched pretty thin). You've decided to use a 2-by-2 table to help her reach a decision. On a separate piece of paper construct this table and make at least two sample entries in each of the four boxes.

7. What decisions are now being made by work groups or individuals that were formerly made at higher levels of management?

8. What decisions are now being made by management or technical experts that you feel could be made by empowered teams or individuals, given proper training and support?

Appendix

The following pages are referred to throughout the text. They include forms, assessments, and illustrations of concepts discussed earlier. Each of these items is available in packs of 20 copies from the organization that created them: Training House, P.O. Box 3090, Princeton, NJ 08543. Telephone (609) 452-1505.

Process Skills for Facilitators

Directions: Your job is to enter a number from 1 to 5 in each of the two columns to the right of each statement, indicating the degree to which it applies to your role as facilitator. A 5 is the highest rating and means extremely while a 1 means little if any. The first column indicates the relevance of each skill—its importance to your work as a facilitator. The second column indicates your proficiency—how good you are in applying this skill.

                                                                              Relevance Proficiency

1. Skill in leading group discussion by getting full participation, agreeing on purpose and outcome, cultivating commitment, and using the tools of summarizing, probing, recording, testing for consensus, and bringing the discussion to acceptable closure.
2. Skill in collecting and presenting information by researching existing sources, generating new information (conducting surveys and interviews), displaying and interpreting data, and suggesting conclusions and actions when appropriate.
3. Skill in asking questions by using directive and nondirective techniques to elicit facts and feelings (unbiased, complete, and relevant) and, where appropriate, to lead others to come to conclusions and insights for themselves (e.g., in coaching, counseling, and problem solving).

| | Rel. | Pro. |

 4. Skill in listening analytically by interpreting what is and isn't said, by focusing on process and content, by forming hypotheses and testing them, by restating to confirm understanding, and by retaining for subsequent recall. ___ ___
 5. Skill in conducting meetings by informing participants in advance of objectives, agenda, and assignments; by controlling interruptions and digressions; by maintaining the balance of content and process; by using appropriate resources (i.e., people and documents); and by reaching closure on goals. ___ ___
 6. Skill in negotiating and resolving conflict by assessing barriers, determining what is and isn't negotiable, developing alternative strategies, converting win-lose situation to win-win outcomes, and reaching agreement on who will do what. ___ ___
 7. Skill in making presentations by establishing expectancies and purpose, maintaining interest, balancing technical expertise against the group's need to know, converting features to benefits, eliciting participation and feedback, and meeting the objectives of the presentation. ___ ___
 8. Skill in counseling and consulting by analyzing needs, determining resources, exploring options, asking relevant questions deductively, and leading the client to develop appropriate plans of action and to take responsibility for the results. ___ ___
 9. Skill in visualizing and presenting goals by translating organizational and individual needs into challenges that are seen as achievable, important, and exciting, and that are broken down into milestones and subgoals, along with a system for tracking progress. ___ ___
10. Skill in recognizing performance in groups and individuals by establishing accountability and reinforcing significant achievements through individual recognition, celebration, and the management of a system of ongoing feedback. ___ ___
11. Skill in maintaining commitment once the initial excitement and interest in a new program has subsided, by providing variety and new challenges that require individuals and groups to stretch and to flex muscles that have not been used sufficiently. ___ ___
12. Skill in developing teamwork by matching tasks to talents, by helping groups to recognize and draw on the unique strengths of different members, and by reinforcing the importance of individual achievement in support of team goals. ___ ___
13. Skill in communicating trust by being open and candid, by avoiding playing games and politics, and by giving and getting information in simple terms (i.e., in concrete, specific, everyday language rather than jargon or academic vocabulary). ___ ___
14. Skill in developing self-sufficiency by strengthening the confidence and competence of individuals and groups to function more autonomously, thereby weaning them from heavy dependence on outside sources of

	Rel.	Pro.

authority to govern their behavior (including your own efforts as facilitator). ____ ____

15. Skill in solving problems by identifying the deviations to desired performance, separating symptoms from root causes, generating alternative solutions, involving the affected parties, selecting the most appropriate course of action, implementing it, and tracking and fine-tuning results. ____ ____
16. Skill in making decisions by determining whose decision it is (immediacy versus commitment versus expertise versus responsibility for results), generating options, establishing limits (musts) and qualities (desirables), assigning weights, using a decision matrix, assessing risk, and selecting the highest-ranking option. ____ ____
17. Skill in coaching and mentoring by making assignments, giving training, preparing individual development plans jointly, developing materials (e.g., job aids, flowcharts, checklists, or procedures), and providing reinforcement for new behaviors (performance maintenance system). ____ ____
18. Skill in managing projects by defining outcomes, identifying resources, selecting people (the project team), defining roles and responsibilities, planning and scheduling activities in series and parallel, and controlling barriers (i.e., managing the "critical path" on time & budget). ____ ____
19. Skill in documenting and recording by writing in a crisp, complete, reader-friendly format; by setting up appropriate files and systems for storing and retrieving; and by generating proposals, memos, letters, and reports that achieve their intended results. ____ ____
20. Skill in influencing others in groups and individually to implement change by applying the principles of organizational behavior and group dynamics; by assessing the style, motives, drives, and needs of individuals; and by implementing effective actions (strategies, interventions). ____ ____

Total (out of a maximum of 100 points). ____ ____

Guidelines for Group Behavior in Meetings

1. At the start of any meeting, it is essential that the group agree on the objectives (i.e., the purpose and goal) of the meeting. This often means devoting time to a brief discussion of expectations, desired outcomes, and how the group will know that the objectives have been met. It's a good idea to have these expected outcomes written down in brief, crisp wording—on the premeeting announcement, a hand-

out, or a flipchart. At any time during the meeting that any member is confused or has reason to question the relevance of what is being discussed, he or she should ask how it relates to the objectives of the meeting.

2. If participants are new to one another and have not functioned as a group before, it is appropriate to spend a few minutes at the start of a meeting to establish the ground rules. This page is a tool for reaching agreement on the procedure to be used in dealing with issues, maintaining order, and reaching the objectives.

3. Everyone in the group has an equal right to his or her opinion. Members owe one another the courtesy of listening objectively and hearing out all relevant contributions before taking action or attempting to reach consensus.

4. Any member who feels that another member has been cut off, misunderstood, or not given a fair hearing, should bring this observation to the group's attention and return the discussion to the member who was cut off.

5. On the other hand, any member who feels that another member's behavior is counter-productive (e.g., digressing, confusing the issue, making irrelevant comments, or otherwise interfering with the group's timely progress toward the objectives) should attempt to bring the member back into the fold or to find out if other members see the behavior as disruptive.

6. Any member wishing to speak should be first recognized by the leader. This is not always practical (e.g., when discussion is rolling and highly interactive), so the leader and members reserve the right to interrupt and identify the persons whom the group wants to hear. (Without this option, no one will be heard if the group lapses into a verbal free for all.)

7. Feedback is essential if people are to know how their comments are received—especially if there is doubt as to whether the group understood. It is appropriate for anyone to give a member feedback; for example: Let me see if I understand the point you're making, Fred. You seem to be saying that . . . .

8. Any member who feels that the process is not supporting the objectives of the meeting should share this observation—whether privately with the leader or publicly with the full group, whichever is appropriate; for example: if the group wants to reach a decision without hearing the facts or discussing all the options, any member who recognizes this should bring it to the group's attention and not simply go along with the others.

9. All members are responsible for managing group time effectively. Everyone should have an equal opportunity to speak. No one should dominate or monopolize. If too much time is being spent on an issue, anyone can point this out and ask if others agree.

10. Group members have two major reasons for contributing at meetings: they have input to share (fact and opinion) or they are affected by the output of the meeting (decisions reached, actions taken). Members should keep these in mind in determining when and how to contribute.

Sample Response Sheet: Training Session on Instructional Skills

The effective instructor functions as a catalyst. Recalling your past courses in the sciences, see if you can list two qualities of a catalyst that are also qualities of an effective instructor:

Starting a New Class

During the initial half hour or so of any new class, the participants want to know the answers to four major questions. What are they? We'll get you started with the first word of each. Here they are:

Who

Why

What

How

Nervousness

Anyone who has a professional pride in their work is likely to be nervous when faced with the responsibility of performing in front of a group. Athletes, entertainers, courtroom lawyers, actors on opening night, public speakers, and even instructors. What are some of the things we can do as instructors to reduce and control our nervousness at the start of a course?

-
-
-
-

Divide and Conquer

There are many benefits of having participants work in pairs or small subgroups during a class. See if you can list at least six in the space below.

-
-
-
-
-
-

The S-R-F Model

Anything we show or tell our learners is the stimulus. Anything we get the learner to do to show understanding is the response. And any information the learner gets to confirm or correct the Response is the feedback. This S-R-F model (Figure A.1) is the smallest unit of instruction.

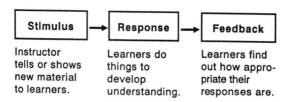

Stimulus	Response	Feedback
Instructor tells or shows new material to learners.	Learners do things to develop understanding.	Learners find out how appropriate their responses are.

Figure A.1

- Why do effective instructors elicit many responses in class? Why not simply fill the class time with stimulus and cover that much more material?
- What are some of the ways instructors can get responses from participants besides calling on individuals to answer questions?
- During a one hour block of instruction, how many S-R-F units do you think is a desirable goal to work toward?_____. How many have we had so far during this session?_____. How many do you think you have in one hour of your instruction of a typical class?_____.

Using Questions Effectively

Questions are our most useful tool for eliciting responses. They can be used to confirm understanding (get information) or to create understanding (give information). In Figure A.2, give at least one example of each type of question. We'll get you started.

Questions Used to Get Information	Questions Used to Give Information
• In Herzberg's motivation theory, is pay a "hygiene factor" (maintainer) or a motivator? Why? • • •	• Do you think that our employees are only interested in the size of their paycheck? • • •

Figure A.2

Getting Relevant Responses from All Participants

- When we pose a question, we are likely to get a reply. But it may not be the response we were looking for (that will help to move the class toward meeting the learning objectives). What are some of the things (at least three) we can do to convert a reply to a response without embarrassing the participant?
- Why do 80% of the responses in class come from the same 20% of the learners, and what are some of the things (at least five) we can do to get all participants giving responses?

A Facilitator's Creed

I believe that an empowered work force can perform at higher levels of productivity, quality, and satisfaction. My role as facilitator is to help other people and the organization meet their goals and accelerate their growth and development.

To accomplish these common goals, I recognize the importance of applying certain concepts and skills in my work. More specifically, I will strive to:

- Determine the goals and desired outcomes of others with whom I work and agree on mutually acceptable ways to meet these goals. This discussion must occur before we undertake a plan of action.

- Identify the stakeholders (i.e., other persons who have input or are affected by the output) of any major actions I might undertake, to solicit their involvement and support from the start.

- Cultivate champions (i.e., influential persons whose advocacy is important to the effectiveness of our actions) and draw on their support as needed without overreliance on their influence or authority.

- Develop action plans and timetables in concept with stakeholders and champions to draw on a rich reservoir of creativity and obtain a deeper commitment. This will require more time and patience than if I work alone, but I believe the results more than justify the extra effort.

- Serve as a mentor to others, coaching and developing them to fuller use of their abilities by avoiding the temptation to give advice and hand out quick-fix solutions.

- Use questions deductively to lead others to think and act for themselves, thereby developing in them the confidence and competence to be more productive, more self-sufficient, and more satisfied in their work.

- Avoid parent-to-child relationships (criticizing and giving advice) by converting such interactions to an adult-to-adult basis (by showing empathy and asking questions, and by maintaining adult transactions in communications that I initiate).

- Plan my actions to release the energy and ability in other persons, thereby enabling (empowering) every employee with whom I deal to be a manager of their own time and talent. This is the full meaning of empowerment, and of my role in facilitating it.

Appendix

MEETING ANNOUNCEMENT/AGENDA

Subject: _____
Today's Date: _____
Meeting Date/Time: _____
Duration: _____
Place: _____
Confirm by Calling: _____

Meeting Leaders: _____
_____

Participants:

Desired Outcomes:

Background Materials:

Please Bring:

Order of Agenda Items	Persons Responsible	Process	Time Allocated

From Managing to Empowering

MEETING RECAP

Subject: _____
Date of Meeting: _____
Recap Prepared by: _____

Participants:

Additional Copies to:

Content Summary:

Decisions Reached:

Actions to be Taken	By Whom	When

174

Appendix

COACHING AND COUNSELING PLANNING SHEET

1. What is the situation in brief?

One of our managers, Mr. Sewell, called to report that Ted refused to expedite an order for one of his people, Mario. Ted is a good man, but doesn't always handle orders in the sequence they come in. He's not as well organized as he should be, and therefore may get shaken under pressure.

2. What are my objectives? What am I trying to accomplish?

1. To get the immediate problem solved — the order sent to Mario.
2. To address the long-range problem — getting organized and prioritizing the handling of orders.
3. To accomplish this in a way that is supportive of Ted and that doesn't add fuel to the fire.

3. How will I know I've succeeded? What evidence will I look for to tell me that I can conclude the session?

I want Ted to see the need for actions 1 and 2 noted above, and to accept them — perhaps even come up with them himself, if I can stay in a nondirective mode and adult to adult.

Ultimately, I'll know I've succeeded when Ted gets the order to Mario and sets up a system for prioritizing the orders.

Copyright © 1991 by Training House, Inc. All rights reserved.

| 4 | What are the objectives of the other person likely to be? What does he/she want to accomplish? |

Ted probably knows that he shouldn't have blown up and shouted at Mario. As soon as I bring up the situation, he's likely to apologetic and defensive, and will want to get me off his back. However, my accepting of his apology won't solve the problem — at least not long range.

| 5 | What specific action do I want each of us to take as a result of this session? |

Ted should get the order to Mario (immediately), and get a system for stamping and prioritizing orders (long range).

I should call Mr. Sewell to apologize and to tell him the order is on the way. I could also have Ted call him, but that strikes me as punitive — Parent to child. In addition, Mr. Sewell called me, not Ted. I don't want to risk having him bent out of shape.

| 6 | What time frame is needed to carry out these actions? |

Get order to Mario within the next two hours.

Have new system in place by the end of next week.

Appendix

7 — What information do I want to give?

> A. Mr. Sewell called, unhappy.
> B. I know you're quite busy; big backlog.
> C. I want to support you and help you avoid future problems.

8 — What information do I have to get?

> A. Why did you refuse?
> B. What caused the problem?
> C. How can we avoid future occurrences?
> D. What shall I tell Mr. Sewell?
>
> (These questions must be asked in a supportive, non-directive manner — not as stated here.)

9 — What is my strategy, or game plan, for the giving and getting of information noted in 7 and 8 above? That is, in what sequence do I give and get?

> I will listen first and avoid passing judgement. After we've agreed on the problem, I'll get Ted to work out the solution. Here is my sequence for giving and getting the information noted above:
>
> 7A – 8A – 8B – 7B – 7C – 8C – 8D

10 (To be completed after the session.) How did it turn out? What did I learn about counseling and coaching that will influence my next session (either with this person or another one)?

Session turned out better than expected. Ted was cooperative and is going to work up a system for stamping and prioritizing orders in the future.

What did I learn? My natural tendency is to be very directive: Do this, this, and that, and do it now — sort of a shoot-first-and-ask-questions-later style. I had to resist the temptation to chew Ted out and tell him what I want done. But I can see from this session that my old style is not as effective as drawing Ted out and getting him to work out the solution. I'm still not comfortable with the new style (it's not natural), but if it works, I'll stick with it!

Appendix

Team Member's Creed

I believe that teamwork is essential if we are to fulfill our mission and to meet or exceed our customer's requirements and expectations relative to productivity, quality, service, and cost.

To accomplish these common goals, all team members must be willing to show initiative, contribute their full potential to whatever they undertake, and act with integrity at all times. As team members, we must continuously strive to work together, listen and talk effectively, learn and apply new skills, and enjoy the satisfaction of performing as a finely-tuned natural work group.

More specifically, we believe that we must:

- Understand and share in the goals of the organization.
- Accept responsibility and be accountable for the results we obtain.
- Be listened to by management and work to cultivate their full support.
- Communicate openly and support one another, within and outside the team.
- Work to build and maintain mutual understanding and trust.

These factors are our responsibility as team members—the result of our commitment to teamwork. We recognize that for team members to contribute their full potential, we require the following support:

- Regular establishment of goals, standards, and priorities.
- Prompt and specific feedback and recognition on the results of our efforts.
- Training and learning opportunities that enable us to apply new skills.
- Authority and resources as needed to achieve our goals and standards.
- The confidence and support of all parties with whom we work.

INDEX

Achiever types, 85
Acquisition model, 128
Action initiation, 75, 77
A-D-A model, 128–29
Administrative competencies, 27, 28
Adult-to-adult relationships, 3, 9, 17, 19
 and corporate culture, 25, 27, 28–31
 and effective questions, 56
 and meeting leaders, 118
 and work teams, 92
Advising response, 15, 57
Application model, 128
Attitudes, 9, 91, 121, 126, 127, 133
Awareness training, 101

Behavior, 73, 96, 126, 127, 129–30
 guidelines for, 167–69
Benchmarking, 2, 3, 90
Benevolent paternalism, 24
Binary decisions, 160–61
Boeing Corporation, 5
Bottoms-up management, 23
Brush Wellman Company, 5
Buddy system, 100

Catharsis, 133
Chairperson, 111
Champions, 2
Chart. *See* Organization chart

Child-to-parent responses, 18, 92
 see also Adult-to-adult relationships; Parent-to-child relationships
CIPs. *See* Continuous improvement programs
Clarification, rephrasing and, 51–52, 70
Climate setting, 40
Coaching and counseling, 58, 133–41
 constructive feedback, 138–39
 functions, 134
 guidelines, 136–38
 planning sheet, 175–78
 planning steps, 135–36
 self-quiz, 139–41
Coca-Cola Companies, 5
Cognitive competencies, 27, 29
Commitment, 133, 155
Communication competencies, 27, 30
Communication styles, 19–20
Competencies
 administrative, 27, 28
 cognitive, 27, 29
 communication, 27, 30
 supervision, 27, 31
 task, 27, 88
Concept to customer (CTC) program, 5
Content issues, 73, 111–12

Continuous improvement programs (CIPs), 2, 90
Corporate culture, 4, 10, 23–34
 organizational behavior, 92–94, 104
 self-quiz, 32–34
 ship metaphor, 3, 4, 91
 Theory X vs. Theory Y charts, 26, 28–31
 and work teams, 91
Counseling. *See* Coaching and counseling
Creeds, 6, 179
Critical response, 15, 57
CTC program. *See* Concept to customer (CTC) program

Decision making, 151–63
 binary, 160–61
 car-buying example, 157–60
 conditions, 151
 problem solving compared with, 153–55
 self-quiz, 161–63
 types of, 152, 153, 155–56
Decision matrix, 158–59
Deflecting and returning, 70–71
Demonstration model, 128
Development. *See* Training and development
Directive questions, 40, 50, 53

181

Discussion leadership skills, 35–47
  roles and responsibilities, 37–45, 53, 67, 78
  self-quiz, 45–47
  see also Meeting leadership
Drucker, Peter, 153

Ego states, 16–19
Empathic response, 15, 56
Employee involvement, 9, 95
Empowerment and facilitation, 1–7
  definitions, 2, 4, 6, 53
  reasons for, 3
  self-quiz, 6–7
  types of, 2–3, 39
  workshop examples, 4–5
  and work teams, 92–93, 95, 96, 97, 101
  see also Facilitators
EXCEL facilitation skills, 5
Expertise, 155

Face saving, 38
Facilitation skills. *See* Discussion leader skills; Meeting leadership; Empowerment and facilitation; Leadership roles and responsibilities
Facilitators, 2, 6, 53, 110
  counseling session role, 134
  process skills for, 165–68
Facilitator's Creed, 6
Feedback, 63–66, 95, 127, 138–39, 173
Flowchart analysis, 145–46
Follett, Mary Parker, 107
Ford, Henry, 86
Ford Motor Company, 5
Forming, 87, 88
Four Ps, 113

General Electric Corporation, 6

George, Howard, 5
Goal setting, 68–69, 101–3, 104
Group member, 110–11
Group size, 42
Groups. *See* Self-directed teams; Work teams

Hard Theory X, 4, 20, 24, 92
Hard work, 24
Hierarchical organization chart, 86, 87
High achiever, 85
How to Make Meetings Work (Doyle & Straus), 110
Human Resources Development (HRD), 2
Humor, 45

IBM Corporation, 5
Inconsistent viewpoints, 38
Information flow, 35
Instructional chain, 127–28
Integrating and focusing, 69
Interaction Method, 110–11
Inventory taking, 40–41

Japanese companies, 93
Job satisfaction, 102
Joint decisions, 155
Judge or referee role, 44
Judgmental parent, 16–17, 20, 92

Kennedy, John F., 86
Knowledge, 9, 121, 126, 127

Leadership roles and responsibilities, 67–83
  deflecting and returning, 70–71
  goal setting, 68–69
  increasing participation, 73, 74
  initiating action, 75, 77
  integrating and focusing, 69
  problem participants, 79–80

Leadership roles (*cont.*)
  rephrasing and clarifying, 70
  as resource, 77–78
  self-quiz, 81–83
  setting limits, 73
  structuring, 78–79
  summarizing and follow up, 80–81
  tension release, 71–72
  work teams, 88, 97–99, 104
  see also Discussion leadership skills; Meeting leadership
Leading Edge Action Program (LEAP), 5
Learning, 121, 125–29
Limit setting, 73
Low achiever, 85

Malaysian Airlines System (MAS), 23
Management
  and meeting leadership, 111
  styles, 10, 19–20
  Theory X vs. Theory Y, 27, 28–31
  total quality (TQM), 2, 3, 5, 9, 90
  and work teams, 91, 94–97, 99–100, 104
Managerial Grid, The (Blake & Mouton), 111
MAP assessment program, 5
Matrix organization, 17–18, 86, 87
McGregor, Douglas, 4, 20, 25
Meeting leadership, 107–20
  objectives, 108–10
  problems, 112–19
  process and content, 111–12
  roles and responsibilities, 110–11
  self-quiz, 119–20
  see also Discussion leadership skills

182

Meetings
  announcement/agenda form, 74, 173
  behavior guidelines, 168–72
  recap form, 76, 174
  summarizing and follow up, 80–81
  work teams, 98–99
Membership roles, 88–89, 97–99, 104, 110–11
Mentoring, 2, 3
Middle management, 3
Milestone recording, 38–39

Non-directive questions, 40, 53
Norming, 87, 88–89
Nurturing parent, 16–17, 20, 92

Objective setting, 37–38, 108–10
Opinions, 40
Organization. *See* Corporate culture
Organizational behavior, 92–94, 104
Organization chart, 3, 17–18, 86–87
Output, 133

Parental types, 16–17
Parent-to-child relationships, 3, 4
  child-to-parent response, 18, 92
  and corporate culture, 24, 25, 27, 28–31
  and effective questions, 57
  and meeting leadership, 118
  as response style, 9, 17, 19, 20
  and work teams, 91, 92
Participation levels, 40, 42, 73, 74, 155
People
  assumptions about, 26
  competencies, 27, 88

Performance, 87, 89–90, 133
Performance deficiency, 145–46
Personal opinions, 40
Planning phases, 39
Problem analysis, 154
Problem participants, 79–80
Problem solving, 39, 143–49
  decision making compared with, 153–55
  flowchart analysis, 145–46
  overview, 147
  self-quiz, 148–49
Procedural issues, 73
Process skills, 89, 165–67
Process vs. content, 111–12
Public Service Electric and Gas (PSE&G), 5–6
Pygmalion effect, 20

Quality, 155
  see also Total quality management (TQM)
Questions, 49–66
  avoiding bias, 52–53
  effective asking, 53–57, 173–74
  evaluation and feedback, 63–66
  purpose of, 57–58
  restating and clarifying, 51–52
  self-quiz, 58–61
  types of, 40, 50–51, 53
  use of, 78

Recorder role, 110
Referee or judge role, 44
Regrouping, 43
Rephrasing and clarifying, 51–52, 70
  see also Summarizing techniques
Resources, 77–78
Response, 127, 173
Response style, 9–21
  and effective questions, 56–57
  interpreting, 15–19

Response style (*cont.*)
  self-assessment exercise, 10–14
  self-quiz, 20–21
  work teams, 92
Responsibility sharing, 41, 101–3, 104
Results-oriented objectives, 108–10
Reward structures, 94
Roles and responsibilities. *See* Leadership roles and responsibilities
Routine decisions, 155
Rules formation, 39

Sale and receipt, 128
SDTs. *See* Self-directed teams
Searching response, 15, 56
Self-directed teams (SDTs), 2–3, 86, 87, 93, 94–95, 96
Self-quiz
  coaching and counseling, 139–41
  corporate culture, 32–34
  decision making, 161–63
  discussion leadership skills, 45–47
  effective questions, 58–61
  empowerment and facilitation, 6–7
  meeting leadership, 119–20
  problem solving, 148–49
  response style, 20–21
  roles and responsibilities, 81–83
  training and development, 131–32
  work teams, 104–5
Skills, 9, 121, 126, 127
Soft Theory X, 4, 20, 24, 92
Soft work, 24
S-R-F model, 127–28, 173
Stakeholders, 2
Statistical process control (SPC), 5, 90
Steering committees, 98

Stimulus, 127, 173
Storming, 87, 89
Strategic decisions, 153
Structuring, 78–79
Summarizing techniques, 41, 69, 80–81
Supervision
   competencies, 27, 31
   and work teams, 94–97, 104

Tactical decisions, 153
Task competencies, 27, 88
Team building, 9, 93–94, 95, 97
Team decisions, 155
Team Member's Creed, 179
Teamwork. *See* Self-directed teams; Work teams
Technical decisions, 155
Tension release, 71–72

Theory X, 4, 20
   and corporate culture, 24, 25, 26, 28–31
   and meeting leadership, 118
Theory Y, 20
   and corporate culture, 25, 26, 28–31
   and meeting leadership, 118
Three Ds, 86
Three Ps, 86
Time budgeting, 38, 41
Total quality management (TQM), 2, 3, 5, 9, 90
Training and development, 121–32
   definition, 121
   desired behavior, 129–30
   failures and weaknesses, 9, 123–25

Training (*cont.*)
   learning principles, 125–29
   response sheet, 169–70
   self-quiz, 131–32
   work teams, 99–101, 104
Tuckman, Bruce, 87

Verb uses, 108, 109, 110
Visualization techniques, 44–45

Weighted decision making, 159–60
Welch, Jack, 6
Work teams, 1, 85–105
   growth stages, 87–90
   key issues, 92–103
   life cycle, 90–92
   self-quiz, 104–5
   see also Self-directed teams
Writing, 69